The Columbia Partnership

FaithSoaring
CHURCHES

A LEARNING EXPERIENCE VERSION

www.FaithSoaringChurches.info

George W. Bullard, Jr.

George W. Bullard Jr.

2 Corinthians 5:7

Isaiah 40:31

LUCAS
PARK
BOOKS

ST. LOUIS, MISSOURI

This book is dedicated to
Lyle E. Schaller
who has been a mentor since I started
reading his books 45 years ago, and
began taking training directly from him
35 years ago. It is Lyle who earlier in my
life urged me to write. My first solo book did not
come out until 2006, which was 20 years
late according to Lyle. I am trying
to catch up, but you can never catch up.
I will always be behind.
Thank you, Lyle. I hear your voice
every day.

Endorsements for This Book and Its Author

I found the book to be a wonderful distillation of what it takes for a church to be powerfully used by God. I liked the idea of a synergy (rather than a competition) between Vision, Relationships, Programs, and Management that must be examined and renewed every few years. The book does not ridicule any of the four qualities, as can happen when some leaders refer to Management as "bean counting", or to Relationships as "touchy-feely". The book addresses in many practical ways the need for churches to examine the four qualities and determine whether the church is *FaithSoaring*, would like to be a *FaithSoaring* Church, or is unwilling to do what it takes to become a *FaithSoaring* Church.

— Danny Langley, Pastor, Crosspointe Meadows Church, Novi MI

I have been working for four years using these ideas in the local church, in almost total isolation. I was surprised at how many ideas I thought I alone was emphasizing (community, calling, creativity, connecting Christians and congregations to their place in the overarching narrative of Scripture). *FaithSoaring* seems to me to be the affirmation of the Holy Spirit bubbling up in diverse places as an affirmation for the church to boldly move forward into a new day.

— Kelli Sorg, Senior Pastor, Trinity United Methodist Church, Troy, NC

Bullard nails it! With clarity and insight this hands-on practitioner has pushed back the fog and shone a bright spotlight on the issues and challenges of becoming a *FaithSoaring* Church. Bullard offers insights into the importance of developing and maintaining that illusive synergy between Vision, Relationships, Programs and Management, and the practical steps to allow the Spirit of God to pull congregations forward into the future that God has for them.

— Terry Branscombe, Pastor, Holy Trinity Congregational Christian Church, Riverview, New Brunswick, Canada

George Bullard has created a most helpful guide for those congregations and leaders who are excited to be on a journey of faith that relies on God's Spirit, and not a textbook, for guidance. *FaithSoaring* is not about size, style, theology, staff, or worship, but about a God-led Vision.

— Bill Klossner, Pastor, Congregational United Church of Christ, Punta Gorda, FL

FaithSoaring Churches is another great work by George Bullard which reveals his passion for churches to become extraordinary churches in a culture which sees the church as very ordinary. The insight presented by George should prove helpful to any pastor who wants to lead an exceptional church.

— Robert Winburn, Senior Pastor, Spring Valley Baptist Church, Columbia, SC

FaithSoaring Churches is a must-read-and-implement book for churches that desire to impact their community or city for Christ. It is a book that every pastor and key church leader who desires to influence the world in a positive way needs to read.

— Bill Barker, National Director, Appalachian Regional Ministry, Hurricane, WV

This book puts into understandable images, concepts that several ministers and I have been tossing around. For me the image of the four qualities in a Lexus SUV and their rightful position of synergy is an amazing picture. I appreciated the continual reminders that we need to return to the leadership of the Holy Spirit. George challenges not just churches but pastors, leadership, regions and entire denominations to discern the call of God and then begin to live that out above our own desires and wants.

— Darren Anderson, Pastor, Hampton Christian Church, Hampton, VA

Cover design: Josh Brickey
Interior design: Connie Hui-Chu Wang

Print: 9781603500227
EPUB: 9781603500234
EPDF: 9781603500241

Published by Lucas Park Books
www.lucasparkbooks.com

Table of Contents

A Learning Experience Version

This edition of **FaithSoaring Churches** is called a Learning Experience Version. What does that mean? It means at least the following things:

1. This is a preliminary edition of this book. Other editions will follow as the presentation of the material matures to a point where a new edition is needed.

2. This is an experimental edition of this book. This material is being shared for individuals, groups, congregations, denominational organizations, and parachurch organizations to experiment and test the material to discover its helpfulness and ways to strengthen it. Periodic webinars and teleconferences will be held for dialogue around the material as real-time learning experiences. These will be announced at www.FaithSoaringChurches.info.

3. This is an evaluation edition of this book. Readers are asked to complete an evaluation of the material in this book. To offer an evaluation, go to www.FaithSoaringChurches.info and click on the evaluation link. People who provide a credible evaluation will be named in the acknowledgment section of a future edition of this book.

4. This is a case study requesting edition of this book. Readers are asked to suggest case studies of congregations and denominational organizations they see as *FaithSoaring.* To provide a case study, go to www.FaithSoaringChurches.info and click on the case study link. People who provide a credible case study will be named in the acknowledgment section of a future edition of this book.

5. This is a dialogical edition of this book. Teleconferences and webinars will be offered that address the material in this book. These will be announced on www.FaithSoaringChurches.info where interested persons can also sign up to receive automatic notices of these teleconferences and webinars. Click on the learning experiences link.

6. In one sense this is an ongoing project that is using a CrowdSourcing process that invites a group of people through an open call to be part of creating, molding, and maturity this manuscript to deepen its value to an increasingly larger audience. If you would like to be part of this crowd, send a request to the author at GBullard@TheColumbiaPartnership.org, and clearly state you want to be part of the *FaithSoaring* Churches Project.

Prelude

This is a book about extraordinary congregations. It is not a book about ordinary congregations. Extraordinary congregations boldly go where they have never gone before. They are *FaithSoaring* Churches.

It takes extraordinary character for a congregation to be *FaithSoaring*. It takes a strong belief in and focus on God's leadership. It takes a willingness to risk. It takes a desire to be bold. It takes deep spiritual faith and the courage to move forward when neither the pathway nor the destination are fully clear. It takes a passion for mission. It takes a conviction that God has a special and unique journey for every congregation. It takes a trust in God's leadership when the congregation gets to a point that it can no longer see the place from which it began its *FaithSoaring* journey, nor see the place to which God is leading it.

It does not take a congregation of a certain size, because any size congregation can be *FaithSoaring*. It does not take a congregation with a certain worship style, because any worship style can be present in a congregation that is *FaithSoaring*. It does not take a congregation with a certain type of pastor, staff, and lay leaders, but rather the pastor, staff, and lay leaders who fit the *FaithSoaring* journey God has for the congregation, and who willingly focus more on the future than on the past. It does not take a congregation with certain theological views, because any genuinely Christ-centered theological perspective that holistically focuses on the Triune God can be present in a *FaithSoaring* congregation.

What is the Essence of This Book?

For those of you who are not sure you want to invest the time in reading the entire book, or who need a peek into what I mean by *FaithSoaring* Churches, or who always read the last chapter of a novel first, here is the essence.

FaithSoaring Churches are captivated by the optimal synergy of Vision, Relationships, Programs, and Management. Four simple qualities. Easy to say. Tough to stay focused on. Tricky to keep in proper synergy. If your congregation will learn how to appropriately focus on these four qualities as led by God, and renew them continually, then you can become and regularly renew your status as a *FaithSoaring* Church.

Being a *FaithSoaring* Church is not a destination. It is a stage through which congregations pass for periods of their long-term journey. Yet, it is a stage they have the opportunity to renew every decade or so when it wanes. God's world is a dynamic world, so every time congregations believe they have arrived they lose their *FaithSoaring* character. If this loss is recognized early then that character can be easily renewed. If recognized late it is difficult to renew.

Are Any of These *FaithSoaring* Churches?

One day I thought about the congregations I have attended on a regular basis during my life of more than 60 years in Raleigh, Baltimore, Philadelphia, Mars Hill, Louisville, Charlotte, Atlanta, Columbia, and Hickory. Their names are Temple, Gregory, Haines Road, Bux-Mont, Mars Hill, Twenty-Third and Broadway, West Side, Providence, Avondale First, Spring Valley, Hickory First, and Forest Hills. In some of these I was a lay leader. In others I was on staff or the pastor. Are any of these *FaithSoaring* Churches?

Some have been *FaithSoaring* for a while. Few have sustained those characteristics for the long-term. Two of these congregations merged out of weakness with another congregation. Two have closed. Several are experiencing significant challenges. A couple of these under challenge were once *FaithSoaring*. Two may be *FaithSoaring* or close to it. But, how can more congregations like these I have loved be *FaithSoaring*?

Why Have I Written This Book?

I have written this book because I want to encourage the development and sustaining of more congregations of exceptional ministry to serve in the spirit of the Great Commission and the Great Commandment. I believe that honors God and builds His kingdom, using congregational forms as the basic building blocks.

I have written this book because I suspect you want to experience the very best in congregational ministry. You do not want to be part of a mediocre congregation, but part of one that soars into the unknown led by the One who knows what is ahead. You want to be the senior or solo pastor, a staff member, or a lay leader or participant in a *FaithSoaring* Church.

For more than 35 years I have worked as a consultant or coach to congregations. I do not know how many congregations I have assisted. But, it is a bunch. Thousands during four decades. I have been on-site with more than 500 congregations. Certainly tens of thousands of congregational leaders have been in the audiences where I have spoken. I have been in a majority of the states in the USA and a majority of the provinces in Canada.

I have been with more than 50 identified denominations from Pentecostal Holiness to Anglican, from Church of God to United Church of Christ, and from Christian and Missionary Alliance to Reformed Church in America. Baptist is my denomination of heritage, so you can probably guess that I have been with a majority of the 35 different Baptist denominations in North America.

In all of these settings I have been passionate about congregations moving towards their full kingdom potential to be *FaithSoaring* Churches. Yet few have. Too many believe that good enough is good enough. Too many lack the faith and trust that God will be with them on a bold journey into the unknown. Too many fail to be passionate about moving in the direction of their full kingdom potential.

Ways to Use This Book

I hope you will use this book to help your congregation engage in *FaithSoaring*. If it is not already a *FaithSoaring* Church, it may yet be.

1. Begin with a personal reading of the book and apply your learnings to your leadership role in your congregation.

2. Church staff teams could use this to assess the situation of your congregation and imagine ways to lead your congregation into the next dimension of ministry.

3. The lay leadership community of your congregation would benefit from studying this book together and implementing a plan to put its principles and strategies into action. Your deacons, session, vestry, council, or board will benefit from dialogue around this book.

4. Small groups and discipleship groups in your congregation may also benefit from studying this book as a group, as it may inspire them to action and reflection.

This book can be the subject of a series of learning experiences in your congregation. It can be the curriculum for an all day workshop with your leadership. It can be the focus of a leadership retreat. It can be the subject of a six to 12 week small group study and dialogue. Or, it can be used in other ways you can imagine

Reading This Book

As you read this book note that at the end of each chapter are some coaching insights and a section for personal reflection. Between chapters is an Interlude that highlights a perspective on *FaithSoaring*.

Part One

Overview of *FaithSoaring* Churches

Part One contains three chapters: Soaring with Faith, *FaithSoaring* Churches, and *FaithSoaring* Churches Characteristics. It provides for the reader basic understandings about *FaithSoaring* Churches, and provides a conceptual foundation for dialogue in the next part around the qualities of *FaithSoaring* Churches.

Here is a brief executive summary for each chapter.

Chapter One: Soaring with Faith

This first chapter provides a definition of *FaithSoaring* Churches. It then goes beyond that to suggest other frameworks or categories that begin to indicate when a congregation might be considered a *FaithSoaring* Church.

The most important part of this chapter beyond the definition is the declaration that *FaithSoaring* Churches have a synergy of Vision, Relationships, Programs, and Management. Without this synergy there is no *FaithSoaring*.

Chapter Two: *FaithSoaring* Churches

This chapter introduces you to seven congregations who are *FaithSoaring* Churches, once were *FaithSoaring* Churches, never have been *FaithSoaring* Churches, or are striving to be *FaithSoaring* Churches. These congregations will be referred to throughout the book. You may find yourself revisiting these introductions frequently.

Chapter Three: *FaithSoaring* Churches Characteristics

This chapter reviews ten characteristics of *FaithSoaring* Churches, followed by a list of five aspects not necessarily characteristic of *FaithSoaring* Churches.

CHAPTER ONE

Soaring with Faith

West Side was an unlikely *FaithSoaring* Church when I became its part-time Community Minister 40 years ago while working on my seminary degree. In fact, during the previous three to five years it had considered closing several times. Located in an upper lower class to lower middle class inner city neighborhood, West Side had been in significant decline for 20 years. At its height it had 550 in attendance. At its lowest it had 55.

Two years earlier a seminary graduate student had been called as pastor. After he had been there for around a year the chairperson of the pastor search committee revealed that he was ninth on their list of nine candidates for pastor. The first eight told them they ought to close. He was the only one did not mention this. The committee took this as a sign that he was the right person to be their pastor.

This new pastor, Robert, was great with Relationships, a good preacher and teacher, and desirous of casting Vision. He was very right-brained. However, he was not gifted in Programs and Management. One of the things I brought to the team was a strong focus on Programs and Management, and a left-brained focus. Robert and I connected well. I am not sure we knew what we were doing, but we were willing to try most anything.

In the two years before I came Robert had done an outstanding job of building up the Relationships within the congregation and in its geographic context. He was an excellent pastor to many people who had felt disenfranchised by the congregation. Attendance was up, the spirit was up, and the readiness of the congregation to address spiritual and strategic issues was apparent.

My role was to develop the church and community connections, and that went well. Robert led the congregation, and sought passionately to cast Vision. They did not hear it. Finally he realized that what he needed to cast was survival. The mantra became one of if we do not reconnect with our community context we are going to die. The congregation heard that and responded to Robert's leadership.

But they never seemed to hear, much less become captivated by, the Vision God was clearly and loudly seeking to impart to the congregation. Before they did, Robert moved on to his first full-time pastorate. I was called as pastor. During my first year something dramatic happened that I call *Harold's Breakthrough Discovery* [See www.ChalicePages.com for a downloadable edition of this story].

In a short period the congregation became captivated by Vision and began moving forward in significant and positive ways. Numerical growth happened. Spiritual growth happened. Missional engagement increased geometrically. Within 12 to 18 months this congregation was *FaithSoaring*. While a lot of human work went into this transformation, it was really the movement of God among the congregation that caused them to be willing to soar with faith.

This is not the end of the story. The challenge for West Side and many other congregations is that *FaithSoaring* characteristics may be experienced, but they also may not be sustained long-term. It took five years from the time Robert came to the congregation as pastor before they could be characterized as *FaithSoaring*. By my observation their *FaithSoaring* status only lasted about three to five years and then it waned. During that time I moved forward into a denominationally-sponsored consulting role with congregations in transition and change situations in large urban areas.

One significant takeaway to remember is that we did not know what we were doing. We did not know what would work. God was in the leadership and we were responding. It is only in reflecting back to this time in the life of the congregation and our ministry that we learned the principles that were at play.

It is from learning these principles that over the years I have constructed a framework and focus I now call *FaithSoaring* Churches. But how should that be defined?

Defining *FaithSoaring* Churches

FaithSoaring Churches are congregations who effectively soar with faith to achieve exceptional ministry.

FaithSoaring Churches are congregations who boldly and effectively soar with faith into a future known only by God where they have never gone before, and which they cannot see at the beginning of their journey.

In greater detail, *FaithSoaring* Churches are congregations who effectively soar with faith beyond ordinary ministry toward extraordinary ministry in a quest to achieve exceptional ministry. They respond to the pulling of God. They journey to places of inspiration, imagination, and innovation. They progress through processes of missional formation and engagement. They continually transform their capacity to reach their full kingdom potential.

They are willing to go to the end of all known light or revelation and leap into the darkness because they know God has gone before them. Leaps of faith and extraordinary commitments are commonplace for *FaithSoaring* Churches. They boldly journey into the future as God reveals the pathway of their journey.

As my colleague in ministry, Leonard Sweet, has said, "To step forth in faith is by definition to step over the line." What is beyond the line is only known by God, and thus involves continual steps of faith by the traveler.

Like Abram in Genesis 12 they gather up their possessions and go on a journey into the unknown because of their faith in God's leadership. They are enabled to soar because of their faith response. They cannot necessarily see the future better than other congregations, but they see clearly with trusting eyes the One who sees the future and draws them toward it.

> **1** Now the LORD said to Abram, "Go forth from your country, And from your relatives, And from your father's house, To the land which I will show you; **2** And I will make you a great nation, And I will bless you, And make your name great; And so you shall be a blessing; **3** And I will bless those who bless you, And the one who curses you I will curse. And in you all the families of the earth will be blessed." [Genesis 12:1-3 NASB]

Like the Israelites after the Exodus 13 their journey is God-led by a cloud by day and fire by night. *FaithSoaring* Churches see clearly, and discern thoroughly the directional signs God has place before them.

> **21** The LORD was going before them in a pillar of cloud by day to lead them on the way, and in a pillar of fire by night to give them light, that they might travel by day and by night. **22** He did not take away the pillar of cloud by day, nor the pillar of fire by night, from before the people. [Exodus 13:21-22 NASB]

Like Gideon in the struggle with the Midianites and the Amalekites in Judges 7 the journey to become *FaithSoaring* is a God-size journey that cannot happen by human effort and should not result in boasting by humankind but a celebration of the glory of God.

> **2** The LORD said to Gideon, "The people who are with you are too many for Me to give Midian into their hands, for Israel would become boastful, saying, ‹My own power has delivered me' [Judges 7:2]

I like to refer to the challenge Gideon faced as a BHAG which I call a Big Holy Almighty Goal. This is inspired by the work of author, teacher, and consultant/coach Jim Collins who uses BHAG to refer to big, hairy audacious goals. I have translated it into biblical talk and hopefully enhanced its meaning.

Like the admonition in Isaiah 40 to wait on the Lord, mount up with wings as eagles, to run and not be faint, *FaithSoaring* Churches soar with wings of eagles.

> **28** Do you not know? Have you not heard? The Everlasting God, the LORD, the Creator of the ends of the earth, does not become weary or tired. His understanding is inscrutable. **29** He gives strength to the weary, and to *him who* lacks might He increases power. **30** Though youths grow weary and tired, and vigorous young men stumble badly, **31** Yet those who wait for the LORD Will gain new strength; They will mount up *with* wings like eagles, They will run and not get tired, They will walk and not become weary. [Isaiah 40:28-31 NASB]

Like the journey of Jesus where by Luke chapters 8 and 9 his focus is on going to Jerusalem after a lifetime of readiness, and on preparing the disciples to carry on His ministry, *FaithSoaring* Churches journey in the direction of the destination for which God has prepared them. Similar to Jesus, they appear to become more aware of God's plan for them as they journey toward the climax of their ministry experience.

> **1** Soon afterwards, He *began* going around from one city and village to another, proclaiming and preaching the kingdom of God. The twelve were with Him, [Luke 8:1 NASB]

> **1** And He called the twelve together, and gave them power and authority over all the demons and to heal diseases. **2** And He sent them out to proclaim the kingdom of God and to perform healing. **3** And He said to them, "Take nothing for *your* journey, neither a staff, nor a bag, nor bread, nor money; and do not *even* have two tunics apiece. **4** Whatever house you enter, stay there until you leave that city. **5** And as for those who do not receive you, as you go out from that city, shake the dust off your feet as a testimony against them." **6** Departing, they *began* going throughout the villages, preaching the gospel and healing everywhere [Luke 9:1-6 NASB].

Like Ananias who responded to the forceful call of God to go minister to Saul whom he considered an enemy, so *FaithSoaring* Churches cross barriers to minister in places and among people where they feel discomfort. As with Ananias, they ultimately realize God is already there and they are simply following His lead.

17 So Ananias departed and entered the house, and after laying his hands on him said, "Brother Saul, the Lord Jesus, who appeared to you on the road by which you were coming, has sent me so that you may regain your sight and be filled with the Holy Spirit." **18** And immediately there fell from his eyes something like scales, and he regained his sight, and he got up and was baptized; and he took food and was strengthened [Acts 9:17-18 NASB].

Like the apostle Paul, *FaithSoaring* Churches venture out on a missionary journey guided by God's Holy Spirit. They remain open to a new Macedonian call such as is recorded in Acts 16. Their life journey has different major phases as is illustrated by the at least three distinct missionary journeys of Paul.

9 A vision appeared to Paul in the night: a man of Macedonia was standing and appealing to him, and saying, "Come over to Macedonia and help us." **10** When he had seen the vision, immediately we sought to go into Macedonia, concluding that God had called us to preach the gospel to them [Acts 16:9-10 NASB].

Who Are *FaithSoaring* Churches?

Faithful, Effective, and Innovative Congregations: For many years I have described what I am now calling *FaithSoaring* Churches as faithful, effective, and innovative congregations. They are faithful to the core Gospel and the ethos of their denomination, affinity movement, or missional journey. They are effective in missional formation and engagement, and pursue excellence at every opportunity. They are innovative and ever changing in methodologies; always seeking new and relevant ways to tell the never changing true story of Jesus.

FaithSoaring Churches are the leading edge congregations in denominations or movements. According to a principle I learned from management guru and churchperson Peter Drucker, they are less than 20 percent of congregations. They must make progress for the other 80 or more percent of congregations, as a group, to make progress. Without the forward movement of *FaithSoaring* Churches there is no overall progress in the full collection of congregations.

Perfecting Congregations: I have also referred to *FaithSoaring* Churches in a typology of congregations as Perfecting congregations. [The other categories are Pursuing, Preparing, Providing, and Presiding and are discussed in my book **Pursuing the Full Kingdom Potential of Your Congregation**. St. Louis: Chalice Press, 2006.] Perfecting congregations are those already on a spiritual and strategic journey to achieve their full kingdom potential. They know who they are, what they value and believe, where they are headed, and how they are getting there. They are simply continually perfecting that journey.

Pursuing congregations are seeking to become *FaithSoaring* Churches, and have the capacity and opportunity to do so. Preparing congregations are seeking to develop the capacity to become Pursuing congregations because they do not yet have what it takes to become *FaithSoaring* Churches. Providing congregations are effective in a limited number of areas of ministry and are generally satisfied with their current situation. For them good enough is good enough. Presiding congregations are carrying out the basic programs and ministries of a congregation, and are unmotivated to do more.

Successful, Significant, and Surrender Congregations: Three words which describe *FaithSoaring* Churches are success, significance, and surrender. They are successful in their kingdom endeavors, but organizational success is not sufficient for them. It is people they want to impact more than numbers they want to acquire. They also address significant spiritual and strategic issues in a manner that brings forth deep transition and change that can lead to continual transformation. They fully surrender to God's leadership as the only leadership that will allow them to soar with faith. As a result they are pulled forward by God's eternal leadership rather than pushed forward by their own limited, finite leadership.

Synergistic Congregations: What I am proposing in this book is that *FaithSoaring* Churches are those with a continually transforming synergy of Vision, Relationships, Programs, and Management. I consider these the four organizing principles of congregations. [I will refer to these as "qualities" throughout the book.] These qualities are simple. Achieving synergy is tougher than it looks.

Synergy occurs when multiple qualities work together to achieve a result that is geometrically greater than the result that any one of them could have achieved independently. In the case of *FaithSoaring* Churches these qualities are Vision, Relationships, Programs, and Management. No one of these qualities, as good as they are, can enable a congregation to soar with faith. It takes a synergy of all four for *FaithSoaring* to be achieved.

These qualities of Vision, Relationships, Programs, and Management also correspond in an analogous way to the qualities stated in Mark 12:30 of heart, soul, mind, and strength.

> **30** And you shall love the Lord your God with all your heart, and with all your soul, and with all your mind, and with all your strength. [Mark 12:30 NASB]

Vision is about heart and deals with core values, passion, causes, and significance. Relationships are about soul and deals with experiences, thrills, and the love of interaction with people. Programs are about mind and deals with strategies, structures, goals, and accomplishment. Management is about strength and deals with actions, efficiency, focus, and metrics.

A Synergy of Vision, Relationships, Programs, and Management

Thus, Vision, Relationships, Programs, and Management individually are not enough. As individual qualities—silos—they cannot help a congregation become a *FaithSoaring* Church. It is only when they work together—become synergistic—that they can help a congregation soar with faith.

Imagine that the journey of your congregation—which I call a Spiritual Strategic Journey or an Experiential Missional Journey—could be characterized as a road trip in a luxury sports utility vehicle. Let's say a Lexus SUV. [Many other types of SUV models could be chosen. A Lexus SUV implies for me the values and excellence of the journey we are discussing.] Then let's suppose the four passengers in the vehicle are Vision, Relationships, Programs, and Management.

Who's driving? In *FaithSoaring* Churches Vision is driving. Who's navigating? Relationships are navigating. Programs are in the back seat behind Relationships providing the programs, ministries, and activities framework within which Relationships can best function. Management is in the back seat behind Vision providing the administrative infrastructure to free Vision to soar like the wind.

Vision is driving because it fuels the journey. Relationships is navigating because it flavors the journey. Programs and Management are in the back seat playing essential supporting roles. All four must be present in the vehicle for a successful and significant journey that ultimately leads to sacrifice in response to God's leading.

The synergy the four passengers can produce is essential to becoming a *FaithSoaring* Church. This means that not only is their presence essential, but where they are seated in the vehicle is non-negotiable for *FaithSoaring* Churches. It is essential that Vision and Relationships are in the front seat. It is essential that Programs and

Management are in the back seat. Further, it is imperative that Management is on the left side behind Vision. It is essential that Programs are on the right side behind Relationships.

The reality is that this ideal configuration that produces synergy is elusive for congregations. It is difficult to achieve. Once achieved it does not usually last more than seven to nine years without intentional action to rebalance Vision, Relationships, Programs, and Management. Without rebalancing, they will be out of balance; they will significantly and negatively impact the journey of a congregation.

Lexus SUV

Vision *Driving*	**Relationships** *Navigating*
Management *Supporting*	**Programs** *Supporting*

Coaching Insights for the Chapter One

Personal Reflections for Learners

In what ways is your congregation a *FaithSoaring* Church?

In what ways is your congregation not currently a *FaithSoaring* Church?

More specifically, in what ways is your congregation faithful, effective, and innovative?

In what ways is your congregation a Perfecting congregation?

In what ways is your congregation one who is significant in the fulfillment of its mission, or even fully surrenders to God's leading?

Where currently is the synergy of Vision, Relationships, Programs, and Management in your congregation?

Your Reflections: **What are your reflections on the material presented in this chapter?**

Your Actions: **What actions do you need to take about your life, ministry, and/or congregation based on this chapter?**

Your Accountability: **How and by whom do you want to be held accountable for taking these actions?**

Interlude

FaithSoaring or Falling?

Karl Wallenda, patriarch of The Flying Wallendas high wire circus act, fell 75 feet to his death March 22, 1978 while walking a cable strung between the two towers of the ten-story Condado Plaza Hotel in San Juan, Puerto Rico.

Reflecting on his death, his widow stated that during the months preceding the fall Karl transitioned from an attitude of confidence and courage, to one of fear and precaution. He morphed from an aerialist who lived to soar, to a hesitant high wire actor who was consumed with the fear of falling.

This fear of falling is now known as The Wallenda Factor. It refers to situations where the fear of failure smothers the joy of soaring. It refers to situations where problem-solving erases affirm and build processes, where counting the "No" votes is more important than counting the "Yes" votes, and negatives are more important than positives.

Too many congregations cannot experience *FaithSoaring* because they are more afraid of falling than they are encouraged to walk by faith rather than by sight. They fear the possibility of failure more than the exhilaration of success. They focus on fixes rather than solutions. They are short-term rather than long-term in their thinking. They do not engage in *FaithSoaring*.

The Wallenda Factor is also expressed in congregations when a threat of some type is present. People are afraid the threat will become a reality, and the congregation will be harmed. Dialogue is often around the possibility of something negative happening to the congregation, rather than the opportunity for *FaithSoaring*.

CHAPTER TWO

FaithSoaring Churches

Who are some *FaithSoaring* Churches? The reality is that they are probably less than 20 percent of the approximately 350,000 congregations in North America. As indicated earlier the ideal configuration that produces the necessary synergy is elusive for the majority of congregations; perhaps upwards to 80 percent of all congregations. Yet it is still a goal congregations ought to strive to achieve.

The seven congregations briefly introduced in this chapter are illustrative of a wide range of congregations seeking to be effective in their setting. Some are soaring with faith and some are not. You may not find in these seven a congregation that exactly fits the situation of your congregation. That is fine as that is not the intention of sharing these seven. From the base of these seven congregations, think through the situation and characteristics of your congregation. How would you describe your congregation?

Further, these are not complete stories. These are just an introduction to these congregations. Use your imagination. Seek to fill in the blanks or missing parts about these congregations. What is your guess about some of the additional details about these congregations? What would you like to know that would illuminate their story and help you to see the story of your congregation?

Summit Heights is a *FaithSoaring* Church. Christ the King is not. Nesmith, a smaller membership congregation, is a *FaithSoaring* Church. Lake Avenue is trying to be. We do not know yet if Midtown will be a *FaithSoaring* Church. Trinity once was a *FaithSoaring* Church, but not anymore. First is struggling to understand what *FaithSoaring* is all about.

Let's look more deeply into the stories of these congregations to suggest how they may or may not fit into the pattern of *FaithSoaring* Churches.

Summit Heights

Summit Heights is almost 27 years old. It began as part of the expansion era of the founding of contemporary congregations during the 1980s. It started with a Boomer generation-oriented style of worship with a seeker-driven focus. It is now past its first generation of life and has matured into being a *FaithSoaring* Church reaching primarily the three birth generations of Boomers, Busters, and Blasters/Millennials.

It conducts worship at one location on the interstate highway outside of town, and in a commercial outlet mall on the other side of town. Total average weekly worship attendance for the two locations is 1,300, yet they count almost 2,800 people as being connected with their congregation. The senior pastor has been with the congregation since it was founded. He preaches at one location, and by video feed at the second location.

Above their base budget of $2.2 million, which includes more than $200,000 for various ministry organizations and their direct missional efforts, the congregation deploys more than 100 people per year outside of North America in various missional engagement projects. Their specialty is providing clean water in Africa.

Mike Martin was the founding pastor of this congregation and has been in the role of Lead Pastor all 27 years. His wife, Cheryl, has been the director of preschool and children ministries since the beginning of the congregation. Other senior staff focus on students, worship arts, administration, disciplemaking, missional engagement, and congregational care.

Christ the King

An ex-neighborhood congregation, Christ the King is not a *FaithSoaring* Church. It probably never was. It was started 43 years ago in a new suburban residential neighborhood. Its primary purpose was to have a congregation of its denomination in a setting where upwards to 20 percent of the residents stated that as their denomination of choice.

It turned out to be a One Generation congregation. This is a congregation that begins with a strong sense of Vision and spiritual strategic direction. It lives into that Vision for up to 22 to 27 years—a generation of time. After that it never quite gets traction. It never redreams it dream. It keeps trying to fix what is wrong so it can go back to the way it was during its first generation.

Its pastor is Gail Jenkins who felt called into ministry at mid-life and came to this church two years ago. She is a wonderful and caring person who leads meaningful liturgical worship, shares thoughtful sermons, and is viewed as very warm and effective in pastoral care. With 135 people in average weekly worship attendance, this almost exclusively Anglo-American congregation contributes well to a $360,000 budget, and keeps the traditions of the congregation moving forward.

Gail Jenkins is the only full-time staff person. Part-time staff focus on music and youth. There is also a person who devotes 20 hours per week to the role of administrative assistant.

Nesmith

"Country Gospel" is an apt descriptor for Nesmith which is definitely a *FaithSoaring* Church. Located in the unincorporated community of Nesmith where there are five Protestant churches, Nesmith congregation soars in missional service. Although during its best years it only averages 55 in weekly worship, it sponsors a Hispanic-American congregation made up of current and former seasonal farm workers from Central and South America, which averages over 100 in weekly attendance.

Almost 20 years ago a laywoman in Nesmith became interested in teaching a husband and wife in the community to read and write beyond a fourth grade level. She discovered their literacy situation when visiting, along with a team from Nesmith, all five totally unchurched households in the community. This family had four children, but their limited education made it difficult for either of them to maintain skilled jobs that produced enough money to support their family.

After building a relationship with the family, and taking training in an adult reading and writing system, this lay leader offered to teach the husband and wife to read and write. They accepted. Over the next 18 months, using a simplified version of the New Testament as parallel reading, she raised their reading and writing skills to an eighth grade level. In the process she had natural opportunities to respond to their questions about faith, the Bible, and Jesus. The result was the beginning of a Christ-centered spiritual journey for the entire household.

Later Nesmith realized that English as a Second Language was a related ministry and that several thousand seasonal farm workers were in their county, and many wanted to learn English, establish permanent residency, and become citizens. With the help of almost a dozen other congregations in the county, Nesmith established what became a large English as a Second Language ministry a decade ago.

Glenn Thompson is the pastor. He is bi-vocational. His other work is as principal of a middle school in the county. All other staff functions are handled by volunteers. The approximate annual income of $110,000 does not allow for additional paid staff.

Lake Avenue

This "Urban Gospel" congregation composed primarily of African-Americans is pursuing a journey that may well lead to Lake Avenue becoming a *FaithSoaring* Church. It was not founded as an African-American congregation. It was founded by Anglo-American families in the mid-1950s in the suburban area of a large city.

Towards the end of its first generation of life its context began to change when a historically black state university built a satellite campus across the street from the church facilities. With significant state and federal government funding, this satellite campus began to expand and rapidly increase in student enrollment.

For several years, Lake Avenue sought to continue the same ministries characteristic of its early years. Ultimately it began a collegiate ministry focused on both the residential and commuting students at the university. They employed two student interns each year to lead the collegiate ministry, but with only limited success.

A hinge point was reached when their pastor of 28 years retired. During the interim the congregation made the decision to pursue an African-American as their next pastor. The result of this pursuit was that they hit the proverbial jackpot. They secured an interracial clergy couple as their next pastoral team. The wife, Joy Goodson, is Anglo-American and the husband, Raymond Goodson, is African-American. While they alternate preaching responsibilities, Raymond is the worship leader each week.

The ministry of the new clergy couple was not immediately effective. Many transition issues needed to be addressed. Their first decade of ministry leadership focused on laying a foundation for excellent ministry. One transition was that the university leapt across the street, and was soon making offers to purchase Lake Avenue facilities. After several rounds of negotiation the offer of the university was accepted, and Lake Avenue purchased and moved into an abandoned strip shopping center a half-mile away.

In their new location Lake Avenue engaged in an extreme congregational makeover. [See www. ExtremeCongregationalMakeover.info.] They started with a blank sheet of paper and redesigned the church. They are now into their seventh year of living into the Vision for a redesigned congregational movement. They are well on their way to becoming a *FaithSoaring* Church with a full synergy of Vision, Relationships, Programs, and Management.

Midtown

At only eight years old, Midtown has not been in existence long enough to fit the definition of a *FaithSoaring* Church. They have not yet developed the formal Management quality in their congregation. It is probably eight or more years away. Yet it certainly is alive with Vision and Programs, and has had great Relationships that it has set aside for a while as it focuses on developing high quality programs, ministries, and activities.

Midtown began in a commercial building near the center of its city. Three clergy families formed the core leadership from the first day forward. One unique element about these families is that one was Asian-American, one African-American, and one Anglo-American. This west coast congregation was multi-ethnic, multi-racial, and multi-cultural from its beginning.

Following a full year of spiritual and strategic preparation, gathering a core community, identifying some Hispanic-American leadership to balance the composition of the clergy staff, they launched with more than 300 people present their first Sunday, and settled into a solid attendance of 260 within the first several months. Now at their eighth anniversary they were averaging 800 in three worship services; one of which is at 9:00 p.m. on Sunday evenings to reach a large collegiate population near the church location.

In keeping with numerical symmetry, they also have eight ministerial and program staff. The lead pastor role is shared by a team of three who with their families and friends founded the congregation. Scott Patton, an Anglo-American, is the Teaching Pastor, Jeremiah White, an African-American, is the Administrative Pastor, and Andrew Lee, an Asian-American, is the Creative Arts Pastor. This multi-ethnic, multi-racial, multi-cultural staff has enabled the congregation to reflect this same nature.

Trinity

Unfortunately Trinity is a former *FaithSoaring* Church. This means they once achieved *FaithSoaring* status, but relaxed thinking that once there meant always there. They did not understand the seven to nine year pattern of *FaithSoaring* that means once a congregation is at least a generation old and Vision wanes for the first time, that any succeeding dream or Vision only has the ability to last seven to nine years before a new transformation effort is needed.

Trinity is 65 years old as a congregation. While it once grew to have 550 in weekly worship attendance, it now vacillates between 80 and 90 in attendance. They have not been *FaithSoaring* for more than 20 years now. A congregation with a worship style seen as traditional within their denomination, they are located in what was once a stable neighborhood two miles from the center of the city, and are now in an ever-changing inner neighborhood. They did not move. The context changed.

Their facilities are aging, and they cannot keep up with the repairs. Once filled classrooms are now used for storage. Their facilities include what was once their first sanctuary, plus the newer, larger one they built three decades ago when they thought they would continue growing. Now they rattle around in it. A Pentecostal congregation uses their old sanctuary and fills their parking lot on Sundays.

Kevin Schmidt has been that Senior Pastor for the past four years. In his late 50s, Kevin left Christian ministry service 13 years earlier following a personally harmful mid-life crisis. Trinity represents his restoration and return to congregational ministry.

First

It is a shame, yet we must admit that First is clueless about what it means to be a *FaithSoaring* Church. It has nothing to do with it being the First church of its denomination in its medium size city. It has to do with its efforts to bring back the 1970s.

First has five birth generations represented in the congregation—Silents, Builders, Boomers, Busters, and Blasters/ Millennials. They have many people with a tenure of membership of 30 years or more. Also, their pattern is that they are almost exclusively attractive to people from a churched culture who understand how church works. Few preChristians and unchurched persons are attracted to, and—unfortunately—welcomed in this congregation. Their worship, discipleship, fellowship, leadership, and missions approaches will be considered cutting edge when the 1970s come back. Until then some call them retro and others reactionary. They have an early Sunday blended worship service that appeals somewhat to the younger and newer people in the congregation. But, the main worship service is at the sacred hour, with the sacred style, and hardly fills half of the 700 seat sanctuary.

Survival is not an issue. They have an annual income of more than $1.3 million from an average attendance in both worship services of 450. Additionally they have a $4 million endowment. With these resources they do not have to be *FaithSoaring*, and there is no danger they will try.

Wendy Gregory is the Senior Pastor of First. She has a PhD in Old Testament Theology. She taught at a denominational seminary before coming to First 21 years ago as Associate Pastor. When the previous pastor left she was called as pastor.

Summary

What is the difference between these seven congregations? What makes one *FaithSoaring* and another not? How can a congregation be *FaithSoaring* at one point, and then lose this characteristic? Hold those thoughts. Let's look first at the characteristics of *FaithSoaring* Churches. Then let's see how these can be applied to these seven congregations. Move forward to chapter three.

Coaching Insights for Chapter Two

Personal Reflections for Learners

Which, if any, of the seven congregations introduced in this chapter is most like your congregation? Which one, if any, is least like your congregation? Is there one in this chapter you would aspire to be like? Why?

If you were to write a similar introduction to your congregation, what would it say?

Your Reflections: What are your reflections on the material presented in this chapter?

Your Actions: What actions do you need to take about your life, ministry, and/or congregation based on the material presented in this chapter?

Your Accountability: How and by whom do you want to be held accountable for taking these actions?

Interlude

FaithSoaring is About Strengthening Relationships

It appears the early decades of the 21ˢᵗ century center around Relationships and building community rather than tasks and maintaining isolation. People want to come together in face-to-face Relationships.

Just as it was felt that the ability to watch your favorite movie in the comfort of your home would mark the beginning of the end of movie theaters, the long-term trends in movie house attendance is up.

In spite of the ability to watch almost every college and NFL football game occurring on Saturdays and Sundays through a special satellite package, the long-term trend is to join your friends in tailgating festivals and watching your favorite team live on location.

Even though radio, television, Internet simulcasts, and digital campuses allow people to enjoy their favorite preacher while reading the Sunday newspaper, people continue to gather in increasing numbers at congregations where deepening relationships with God and one another builds a valuable spiritual community.

For these and other reasons, a top priority of *FaithSoaring* Churches is to strengthen Relationships. One goal should be to broaden and deepen Relationships within the congregation among people of various ages, tenure of connection with the congregation, theological perspective, special ministry interests, worship service attended, and various other characteristics. Not only may unity and harmony be achieved, but also a movement of people may result that will help the congregation leap forward.

Another goal should be to connect with the people, affinity groups, and networks in the context served by your congregation. Strengthening Relationships with the people in your primary context is a very legitimate way to gain an authentic opportunity to talk with their about spiritual issues. When you care about their lives, they will listen to you talk about your faith.

CHAPTER THREE

FaithSoaring Church Characteristics

What are the key characteristics of *FaithSoaring* Churches? Probably there is no perfect set of characteristics. Yet certain key characteristics emerge from my observation of multiple *FaithSoaring* Churches. No two congregations will have the exact same set of characteristics or formula. Each congregation is unique. Will *FaithSoaring* Churches have all of the characteristics presented in this chapter? Many, but not all.

With those brief words, here is one set of top ten characteristics of *FaithSoaring* Churches. Certainly other sets and types of characteristics could be put forth. Consider how many of these are characteristic of your congregation as you review them.

1. *FaithSoaring* Churches walk by faith rather than by sight in the spirit of 2 Corinthians 5:7 and Isaiah 40:31. Second Corinthians 5:7 admonishes us to walk by faith rather than by sight. Isaiah 40:31 challenges us to mount up with wings as eagles and soar. Thus, *FaithSoaring*. One aspect of walking by faith is viewing the congregation in terms of its long-term potential rather than its short-term urgencies. Another is always imagining what is around the corner, over the next hill, or beyond the horizon.

    7 For we walk by faith, not by sight [2 Corinthians 5:7 NASB].

    31 Yet those who wait for the LORD Will gain new strength; They will mount up *with* wings like eagles, They will run and not get tired, They will walk and not become weary [Isaiah 40:31 NASB].

2. Overall they focus more on Visionary Leadership and Relationships Experiences than on Programmatic Emphases and Accountable Management. This also means they focus more on heart and soul than on mind and strength, in the spirit of the Great Commandment in Mark 12:29-31. Yet they have all four—heart, soul, mind, and strength—and have the proper synergy of Vision, Relationships, Programs, and Management.

    29 Jesus answered, "The foremost is, 'HEAR, O ISRAEL! THE LORD OUR GOD IS ONE LORD; **30** AND YOU SHALL LOVE THE LORD YOUR GOD WITH ALL YOUR HEART, AND WITH ALL YOUR SOUL, AND WITH ALL YOUR MIND, AND WITH ALL YOUR STRENGTH.' **31** The second is this, 'YOU SHALL LOVE YOUR NEIGHBOR AS YOURSELF.' There is no other commandment greater than these" [Mark 12:29-31 NASB].

3.   They are captivated by an empowering Vision from God that is cast by leadership and broadly owned throughout the congregation. This Vision fuels and drives them forward toward their full kingdom potential in response to the eternal leadership and pulling of the Triune God. This Vision is not so much a statement as it is a movement to be sensed and experienced. It is not words that are memorized, but a focus and actions that are second nature to the leadership of *FaithSoaring* Churches. A statement or words that are memorized may create an emotional sizzle, but seldom create a passionate and lasting movement.

4.   They focus on congregational strengths rather than weaknesses; what is right rather than wrong; what is good rather than bad; what is loving rather unloving. They do not ignore weaknesses; that is just not where they start. They focus on building the capacities necessary to take the next steps in ministry, and then to sustain these capacities. They are always anticipating the next steps they need to take and projecting the kingdom impact that could come from these steps.

5.   They also have strengths-focused leadership in the spirit of *StandOut* leadership by Marcus Buckingham (the next generation of strengths-based leadership popularized in the *StrengthsFinder* inventory). Strengths are part of the leadership characteristic trilogy of spiritual calling, strengths or skills, and preferences. *StandOut* helps leaders discover their top two strengths and how to enhance leadership practice through a focus on them. [See Marcus Buckingham. ***Standout: The Groundbreaking New Strengths Assessment from the Leader of the Strengths Revolution.*** Nashville: Thomas Nelson, 2011.]

6.   They seek to reach their full kingdom potential by following God's unique leadership of their congregation. Rather than emulating others, they seek to build their own style of *FaithSoaring.* They engage in continual innovation of their style of ministry while retaining their core substance; always seeking to perfect what they are doing to stay on the leading edge of excellence. They pick up principles from other successful, significant, and surrender congregations, but they build a unique approach, based on their community context or target groups.

They pace their execution of transition, change, and innovation in keeping with the speed of organizations who are great by choice. [See Jim Collins and Morten T. Hansen. ***Great by Choice: Uncertainty, Chaos, and Luck—Why Some Thrive Despite Them All.*** New York: Harper Business, 2011.]

7.   They are committed to the highest possible quality age/stage programs, discipleship processes, and missional engagement that meet the real needs of real people in real time. Significant kingdom impact, rather than the success of programs, processes, and engagements is their goal. They desire that the lives of people touched by the activities and ministries of their congregation be spiritually transformed through an ongoing walk with and surrender to the Triune God. They do not over-program their congregation, but focus on what they can do with excellence rather than a long list of things they might do in a mediocre manner with less effectiveness.

8.   They are missional in nature. In fact, it is second nature to them as implied in Matthew 25:31-46. They focus on the expansion and extension of God's kingdom more than on themselves. They focus on going rather than staying. They balance renewing the core of the congregation with extending the ministry globally as well as locally. They are contextually relevant to geographical community, or the target or affinity groups they are called to serve. They are pulled forward by mission, and may even leap across various racial, ethnic, and cultural barriers in prophetic service to others. They realize it is not the joy they experience that matters near as much as the joy in the Lord experienced by those they serve.

9.   They have high expectations of the people connected with the congregation. They seek to engage them in an intentional disciplemaking journey. They ask them for a deep commitment. They expect them to do

four things: (a) attend worship regularly; (b) be in an ongoing discipleship group; (c) build deep friendships both within the congregation for support of what they are doing in the marketplace to be salt and light in God's world; and, (d) to have a place of ongoing service within the congregation or its areas of missional engagement. They know that low expectation congregations never soar with faith.

10. They have worship experiences that are a true encounter with God rather than simply a cultural gathering according to the testimony of people who attend. Worship, as a part of spiritual discernment, is a hallmark of their praise and adoration toward God. Prayer, as an essential part of worshipful relationship and discernment of God's Vision, is of the highest priority in their congregation and not a perfunctory ritual. The Word of God is clearly illuminated in their worship experiences, and applied in their day-to-day lives. Their reputation in their community context as a spiritual place is well known.

Not Necessarily *FaithSoaring* Church Characteristics

Another set of characteristics exist which I call "Not Necessarily *FaithSoaring* Church Characteristics". They are intended to more clearly define who can be considered a *FaithSoaring* Church. Already you may be typecasting or stereotyping who these congregations may be. You are probably wrong at some points and right at others.

1. *FaithSoaring* Churches are not necessarily only large, very large, or mega congregations. They may be. Many in these size categories could be. But size is not a primary criterion. Smaller or medium membership congregations can achieve many or all of the *FaithSoaring* Churches characteristics. This is particularly the case as they are effective in their setting, or with their target or affinity group; especially when the number of households present in their chosen context is small or modest in size. Consider the examples of Nesmith and Trinity congregations.

2. *FaithSoaring* Churches are not necessarily only churches who are evangelistic or seeker-driven, or who reproduce themselves through church planting or a multi-site strategy. Many of these are *FaithSoaring* Churches, and they are an extremely important part of the overall collection of Christian congregations. The key variable is intentionality focusing on living into the God-led Vision for your congregation. Does your congregation have *Vision Plus Intentionality*? If so, that is more the key than is the growth strategy of your congregation. Consider the examples of Lake Avenue and Midtown congregations.

3. *FaithSoaring* Churches are not necessarily of a certain or similar theological or doctrinal persuasion. To say that only pentecostal/charismatic, evangelical, mainline, or liberal congregations can be *FaithSoaring* Churches misses the point. It is more the willingness to be high expectation congregations—those which anticipate that people connected with them grow in the grace and knowledge of Jesus, in the spirit of 2 Peter 3:18. If you are Christ-centered and Trinitarian you most likely fit as a candidate to be a *FaithSoaring* Church.

4. *FaithSoaring* Churches are not necessarily staff-driven congregations. Yes, their senior or solo pastor, and any staff, certainly expresses positive spiritual passion as initiating leaders within the congregation. At the same time, wise staff leaders develop a broad base of ownership throughout the congregation. They realize the congregation will more easily soar if many leaders are developed and empowered to move forward according to their spiritual gifts, strengths and skills, and preferences.

5. *FaithSoaring* Churches do not necessarily have a certain style of worship. The style of worship that helps people connected with the congregation to glory in, focus on, and connect with God, is the right style of worship. This can be contemporary, traditional, praise, liturgical, emergent or alternative, or various other styles. It must be high quality worship that helps people experience and celebrate the presence of God, rather than a cultural gathering where God's presence is incidental.

Coaching Insights for Chapter Three

Personal Reflections for Learners

Which of the ten characteristics of *FaithSoaring* Churches are characteristic of your congregation?

Which are not?

Which characteristics should you pursue next? Why?

What is your reaction to the not necessarily *FaithSoaring* Churches characteristics? Do these sharpen your understanding of *FaithSoaring* Churches, increase the value of such congregations, or dilute the status of these congregations?

Your Reflections: What are your reflections on the material presented in this chapter?

Your Actions: What actions do you need to take about your life, ministry, and/or congregation based on the material presented in this chapter?

Your Accountability: How and by whom do you want to be held accountable for taking these actions?

Interlude

Big Holy Almighty Goals

What will be the numerical strength of our congregation in the year 2050—only 38 years from now?

That answer, of course, depends on many factors, some of which there is no evidence yet in view.

Hopefully, we will be talking not about how we slice our budget pie differently, but how we bake a whole new pie to respond to an emerging global reality and its impact on the work of God's kingdom in our congregation.

We cannot go back to the way things were. We must go forward in the direction of the new things God is doing in His world.

Based on our resources, we must move forward pulled by Big Holy Almighty Goals. For short we can call these BHAG's.* [These are goals so big or so deep we cannot do business as usual and accomplish them. We must do something radically, even prophetic.]

They cannot depend on our own resources. They will happen only because God is in it and we focus our time and energies on responding to His leadership rather than human leadership. They will happen because we do not seek to re-image our congregation in our image, but we all seek to be re-imaged in God's image.

Realistic? No. These are BHAG's. Possible? Only if God leads in this direction and we respond.

*The concept of BHAG's is inspired by Jim Collins in his book, ***Built to Last,*** where he refers to BHAG's using four slightly different words. [See James C. Collins and Jerry I. Porras. ***Built to Last: Successful Habits of Visionary Companies***. New York: Harper Business, 1997.]

Part Two

The Qualities of *FaithSoaring* Churches

The focus of Part Two is on the four qualities of *FaithSoaring* Churches: Vision, Relationships, Programs, and Management. Individual chapters deal with each of these four qualities, followed by a chapter that deals with the interplay or synergy of these four qualities that can produce *FaithSoaring*. A final chapter introduces some strategies for *FaithSoaring*.

Here is a brief executive summary for each chapter.

Chapter Four: The Heart of Vision

This chapter describes the Vision quality, declares Vision is a movement rather than a statement, shares the role of the senior or solo pastor regarding vision, and suggests how you can feel confident that your congregation is captivated by Vision.

Chapter Five: The Soul of Relationships

This chapter describes the Relationships quality. It suggests a process of Christ, Congregation, Community, Calling, and Commission to illustrate the progression of Relationships. It further recommends spirituality, friends, and causes as important parts of 21st century Relationships.

Chapter Six: The Mind of Programs

This chapter describes the Programs quality and how it is the mind element. It then describes the similarities and differences between Relationships and Programs and how they are two sides of the same coin, with Relationships in a lead role and Programs in a support role.

Chapter Seven: The Strength of Management

This chapter describes the Management quality. It is known as the strength element. It must be empowering rather than controlling. Management involves resources, governance, tradition and culture, readiness for transition and change, and operations. Colloquially these are known as *Bodies, Bucks, Boards,* and *Buildings.*

Chapter Eight: *FaithSoaring* Synergy

This is the core chapter that addresses the synergy of Vision, Relationships, Programs, and Management. This synergy must exist for congregations to be *FaithSoaring* Churches. The journey to achieve synergy is recounted by explaining the ten stages of the life cycle of a congregation, and which one or ones represents *FaithSoaring* and what happens when synergy is lost. The image of a Lexus sports utility vehicle is used to describe the needed synergy.

Chapter Nine: *FaithSoaring* Strategies

This chapter looks at some of the pathways to *FaithSoaring*. It begins with understanding the motivation necessary to move toward and sustain a *FaithSoaring* status. It suggests that long-range or strategic planning will not get you there. A Spiritual Strategic Journey or an Experiential Missional Journey may be the sweet spot for congregational efforts. Any effective pathway will lift up the synergy of Vision, Relationships, Programs, and Management.

CHAPTER FOUR

The Heart of Vision

Summit Heights, Lake Avenue, and Midtown have strong Vision. In the past year or two Vision has diminished in Nesmith. Vision is not obvious at the current time in Christ the King, Trinity, and First. It is possible Vision could have diminished by now in Summit Heights since they are at the end of their first generation of life, except for the fact that three years ago they went through an intentional process to re-envision the next 10 years of their life and ministry.

The Vision Quality

The Vision quality is about Visionary Leadership. A statement that initially defines it is as follows: Our congregation has a strong, clear, and passionate sense of our identity involving mission and purpose, our core values, our Vision, and our spiritual strategic journey as a congregation. We know who we are, what we value or believe, where we are headed, and how we are going to get there.

We are confident in God's leadership. Our Vision is God's Vision for us that is continually cast so it might be owned within our congregation. Thus, we have Vision as one of the four qualities, building blocks, or core characteristics for a *FaithSoaring* Church. Specifically, Vision is about heart. Stated in another manner it is the heart of the matter. It is the first quality in the Great Commandment characteristic quartet of heart, soul, mind, and strength.

Does your congregation have a clear, passionate sense of who it is, what it believes or highly values, where it is headed, and how it is getting there? If so, it may have *Vision Plus Intentionality.* This occurs when a congregation has a clear sense of God's Vision for them, and then intentionally align their daily actions to undergird, fulfill, and live into that Vision.

Vision: A Movement; Not a Statement

Vision is not a 15 or less word statement crafted by a committee in the proverbial smoke-filled back room, approved by the congregation or its board, printed on the worship folder, and recited on cue in worship services and other gatherings of the congregation. That is a vision statement. Any similarity between a vision statement and true Vision is purely accidental.

Vision is a movement of God that is memorable rather than a statement by humankind that is memorized. Let's say that again for emphasis: Vision is a movement of God that is memorable rather than a statement by humankind that is memorized. Congregational leadership casts and casts vision until the congregation is captivated by it. Vision is not something you catch. It is something by which you are caught. You are caught up in Vision to a degree that at times you tingle with excitement

Vision is not so much written as it is experienced. Vision must be sensed and experienced within a congregation rather than read or heard. When considering how Vision comes to us, it may be helpful to consider how the gospels in the New Testament came to us. It was first experienced. Then it was reflected upon and shared orally. After a number of years it began to be written down for consistent, accurate sharing of the drama of redemption with everyone who desired to know.

As Vision is experienced, things begin to happen in the direction where God is leading us. We take actions, and then as we reflect on them we wonder if this reflection reveals Vision. As we reflect on the emerging Vision, we share it orally with our full heart, soul, mind, and strength. Ultimately, we write it down to have a consistent historic and dynamic sharing of Vision within the existing and emerging congregation.

Sam Chaise, General Secretary of Canadian Baptist Ministries, posted the following comment about Vision on Facebook December 9, 2011: "At its best a Vision statement captures the essence of the energy that is propelling a community forward. When you're in a community with Vision, you can smell it, taste it, see it, feel it, even before you ever read the Vision statement. It's best to have both Vision and a Vision statement, but if you are only going to have one, go for Vision without the statement."

An Assemblies of God minister, John Bost, says the following about Vision as a movement: "Vision is a spiritual work within the visionaries, a gift of grace. The capacity for Vision can be developed but remains simply a skill set or a propensity until that work of grace. A Vision statement is a great tool to move others toward a time when their hearts become open and their lives receptive to the movement of the Spirit and that prophetic gift of Vision."

T.J. Addington, senior vice president of the Evangelical Free Church of America, said the following about Vision on his Facebook profile on December 6, 2011: "Compelling Vision is a vision that can be articulated clearly, meets real spiritual needs, is other-centered rather than us centered, requires significant energy and even sacrifice to accomplish, and will positively and significantly impact a group, community or area with the love and message of Jesus. Its mandate is one that cannot be ignored."

The Pastor as the Chief Visionary Officer

What is the role of the senior or solo pastor with Vision? This is certainly an issue around which there are various theological interpretations and philosophies of leadership. Here is mine.

God is seeking to impart Vision to the body, the congregation. God is not seeking to impart Vision only to or through the pastor. Yet it is my hope that the senior or solo pastor is among the first, if not the very first, person in the congregation to be captivated by Vision because the pastor has a key role in being the voice of Vision. The pastor through preaching, teaching, and expressions of leadership has the best opportunities to cast and clarify the Vision. He or she is the Chief Visionary Officer or CVO.

Congregations need to free up their pastor to focus on the role of CVO. Pastors, at their best, are uniquely positioned as the spiritual leader of the congregation to champion vision. Researcher George Barna and others have shared out of their research, experience, and anecdotal encounters that only a small percentage of pastors are truly CVOs. Perhaps one reason is that they are smothered in Programs and Management which are not typically the best ways they can add value to the journey of their congregation. Others can lead out in these areas with the encouragement and support of the pastor.

Pastors, for their part, need to distinguish between the Vision God has for the congregation they serve, and the Vision God has for their personal ministry. Often they are not the same. These two come closest when pastors are the founding pastor of a congregation, but even in these cases if the pastor seeks to image the congregation in their image, instead of God's, they may eventually smother the congregation rather than empower the congregation. These two stay distant when a new pastor arrives in a congregation and seeks to reimage the congregation in the image of their personal ministry.

Pastors need to constantly give away or share the Vision with others. The Vision becomes stronger as the pastor continually casts it, and as an increasing number of the people of passion and people of position in their congregation are captivated by the Vision. Pastors who hoard the Vision may be able to push the congregation forward to success, but will seldom lead it to be pulled forward by God to significance, much less to full spiritual surrender. Never will their congregations become *FaithSoaring* Churches if the vision is not deeply and broadly owned throughout the congregation.

Is your pastor truly functioning as a CVO? What can you do as a layperson or staff member to positively support the role of pastor as CVO? In what ways might you be hindering the CVO role of your pastor?

The Congregation and Vision

To be a *FaithSoaring* Church Vision must clearly be owned by the congregation. They must believe Vision comes from God, they need to be captivated by Vision, and they need to be prepared to continually help their senior or solo pastor cast vision.

The congregation must believe Vision involves going forward to the new thing God is doing in and through the congregation. This is as opposed to going back to any previous era during the life of the congregation about which they have great memories. Going forward may seem like an obvious and simple point, however, it is a point many congregation miss. Going back—a four-letter word if you had not noticed—is a place of comfort and where memory of the past makes it seem greater than it probably actually was.

Too many congregations want their pastor to provide Vision. When they are between pastors they want a new pastor who will bring them Vision. When this is their stance, Vision comes and goes with the presence and effective leadership of a pastor. In these cases, when a pastor leaves the congregational Vision also goes out the door.

When I was pastor of an inner city congregation during my seminary years, we worked really hard to help that congregation be vital and vibrant in a community that was dysfunctional and disintegrating. Many of the things we did worked very well.

About eight years after I left the congregation to begin my now more than 35 years of consulting with congregations, I was back at my seminary lecturing for a day on urban ministry. The person who was pastor then asked to meet me for lunch. He was having a really tough time in the congregation. They were not following his leadership and seemed to be going backwards.

He wanted my advice on several issues, and how to deal with a couple of families. He and I saw the family systems of the congregation differently. Therefore, he rejected all of my specific advice. Finally he asked me, "Why did the people love you so much, and hate me so bad?"

I thought for a minute and then I said, "I left! And, if you will leave too the people will begin to increase their love for you." I then went on to explain that while I had a productive ministry in this congregation, it was a rough ministry with as many downs as there were ups. Basically time has healed the downs and the people are remembering the ups. Time had faded their memory, and the "good old days" when I was there were not as good as they remember. They were good, but not that good.

Confident About Vision?

How do you know if your congregation is truly captivated by Vision? Let's suppose that one day you are shopping in a big box store. You are strolling down an aisle casually looking at the items on the shelf when you see a woman pushing a cart down the aisle and coming towards you.

You recognize the woman as someone who has attended your congregation several times recently. Even though you have engaged her in conversation a time or two, you do not remember her name. Do not worry. Although she also recognizes you, she does not remember your name either.

The two of you stop and engage in a conversation. Shortly the conversation turns to church. The woman says, "I am so glad I ran into you today. We have been in town almost eight months, have visited a bunch of churches, and have decided yours is one of our top three. It would be really helpful to me if you could describe what you think is so special about your congregation."

You smile a really big smile. You feel a rush of excitement—that tingle referred to earlier—because you know the answer. Then in your own words you describe the vision of your congregation and how it is living into it.

A few days later you are with a group of friends from your congregation, and you tell them about the encounter in the store. They want to know what you said. You share how you cast the Vision. "Yeah, Yeah," says one of your friends. "That is just about how I say it. I have a special illustration I use, about when my nine-year-old daughter got it about Vision and shared her excitement with me."

If at least 21 percent of the average number of adults present on a weekly basis for worship in your congregation can describe the Vision in a manner that is consistent with many others in the 21 percent, and if every time a major decision comes up in the life of the congregation the question is always asked, "How will this help us fulfill our Vision?," then your congregation is likely captivated by Vision.

To clarify the numerology, if your congregation averages 125 to 135 in weekly worship attendance and 100 of the attendees are adults at least 18 years of age, then 21 percent of these adults is 21 people. For congregations with less than 100 adults in attendance, it is necessary that at least 21 adults are available and do engage in leadership in the congregation for an Enduring Visionary Leadership Community to exist. For congregations with more than 100 adults in average attendance the 21 percent applies and that number increases as the attendance increases.

An Enduring Visionary Leadership Community is an informal concept that talks about the collection of leaders in a congregation whose positive energy, if coalesced, can empower transition and change that may lead to transformation. It is generally composed of the senior or solo pastor, any ministerial or program staff, laypersons with positive spiritual passion about the future of the congregation, and laypersons with positions of formal or informal leadership in the congregation. The number of people must be large enough that it involves the 21 percent or 21 people as indicated above.

The Lasting Power of Vision

How long does a Vision remain active and empowering in a congregation? Probably not as long as the majority of congregations think.

During my growing up years in my parents' home, money was adequate, but at times tight. I can remember my father remarking about the extra money he had to periodically give my mother as she headed to the beauty salon to get a permanent. He felt that a permanent procedure was misnamed. He would say to me, "Son, your mother has to go to the beauty salon to get a permanent. A permanent permanent! Every three months. They ought to call it a temporary."

Being in the zone as a *FaithSoaring* Church involves, among others things, being captivated by Vision. This captivation is not permanent. But it is longer than a temporary. If deeply rooted, the founding dream or Vision of a congregation has the ability to last up to one generation of time, or 22 to 27 years. In a fast changing context, a highly mobile target or affinity group who makes up a congregation, or if major, significant changes happen in the congregation, this can be as short as 15 to 18 years.

Once a congregation is a generation old, and its founding dream or Vision has either been fulfilled or waned in its empowering influence, a new Vision must be cast and must captivate the congregation. Any succeeding dream or Vision, however, only has the ability to captivate the congregation's journey for seven to nine years. Then it also will wane or diminish.

Therefore, every congregation who is more than a generation old must redream its dream and seek a new or renewed Vision and spiritual strategic journey at least every decade. If not it will find itself traveling down the aging side of the congregation life cycle. It can later restore Vision to a driving and fueling role, but it will be harder than if they had seen and responded to the need to do it each decade.

Coaching Insights for Chapter Four

Personal Reflections for Learners

What is the strength and intensity of Vision in your congregation?

To what extent do you have *Vision Plus Intentionality*?

In what ways is Vision a statement in your congregation, and in what ways is Vision a movement?

In what manner does the pastor express the role of Chief Visionary Officer?

In what manner does the congregation own Vision, share Vision, and give evidence of being captivated by Vision?

React to this statement: In *FaithSoaring* Churches Vision is truly a movement of God. Those congregations who have not yet moved into the Vision zone of being a *FaithSoaring* Church must rely on a Vision statement.

Your Reflections: What are your reflections on the material presented in this chapter?

Your Actions: What actions do you need to take about your life, ministry, and/or congregation based on the material presented in this chapter?

Your Accountability: How and by whom do you want to be held accountable for taking these actions?

Interlude

FaithSoaring with Our Strengths

What do you think would make your congregation more successful: improving weaknesses or building on strengths? Unfortunately too many people believe the answer is to improve weaknesses.

This is unfortunate. Improving weaknesses will not help congregations embrace long-term solutions to the opportunities and challenges they face. It will only help them secure short-term fixes. For years several themes of congregational vitality and vibrancy have rung in my ears. One comes from my mentor, Lyle Schaller. He continually says it is important for congregations to affirm what is right and build upon it.

Kennon Callahan is another respected writer, teacher and consultant, most known for his book, **Twelve Keys to an Effective Church**. He declares that if a congregation fixes everything wrong within its fellowship, it would bring itself right up to neutral. It is not the things that are wrong that must be fixed. The focus should be on the things that are right, strong, and have potential to empower *FaithSoaring* Churches.

In their 2001 book, **Now, Discover Your Strengths**, Marcus Buckingham and Donald O. Clifton champion the strengths-based organization that focuses on enhancing its strengths rather than eliminating its weaknesses. It includes an instrument on finding your strengths as leaders so you can focus around talents—*StrengthsFinder* and later *StrengthsFinder* 2.0. From a spiritual perspective, we would talk about focusing on gifts, skills and preferences. *FaithSoaring* is about discovering, discerning, and developing strengths with which to soar in the direction of the full kingdom potential of your congregation. A new instrument called *StandOut* takes this work farther.

[See Kennon L. Callahan. **Twelve Keys to an Effective Church: Strong, Healthy Congregations Living in the Grace of God**. Second Edition. San Francisco: Jossey-Bass, 2010.]

[See Marcus Buckingham and Donald O. Clifton. **Now, Discover Your Strengths**. New York: Free Press, 2001.]

CHAPTER FIVE

The Soul of Relationships

As *FaithSoaring* Churches, Summit Heights and Nesmith have strong Relationships. However, so do Lake Avenue and Trinity. Christ the King, Midtown, and First do not have strong Relationships. In a way it might seem odd that any congregation would be without strong Relationships. Yet, it does happen at various stages of development when a synergy of Vision, Relationships, Programs, and Management does not exist.

The Relationships Quality

Relationships are about Relationship Experiences. A statement that summarizes it is as follows: Our congregation is doing well at attracting people to a Christ-centered faith journey and at helping people who are connected with our congregation to be on an intentional and maturing Christ-centered faith journey. Among the results of the faith journey of people in our congregation is a deepening spirituality, the development of numerous new leaders, and a willingness by many people to get actively involved in congregational leadership positions and in places of program or missional service within and beyond the congregation.

Relationship Experiences cover the processes of evangelism, new member recruitment, assimilation, meaningful fellowship, spiritual growth and discipleship development, and lay mobilization. It includes what is called in some circles the two foci of missional formation and missional engagement. It is the soul of congregations. As heart is to Visionary Leadership, so soul is to Relationship Experiences. *FaithSoaring* Churches place deep emphasis on Vision and Relationships. These two qualities are then the heart and soul of these congregations, and create and sustain the sense of spiritual movement that is essential for these congregations to continue to soar with faith.

Succinctly, Relationship Experiences is best seen as the disciplemaking process in congregations. It is about turning irreligious people into fully devoted followers of Christ. It is about relating people to God, to one another, and to the context in which their community of faith serves. It deals with connecting people to *Christ, Congregation, Community, Calling,* and *Commission.*

Christ

Connecting people with *Christ* most importantly involves the evangelism focus on preChristians who need and desire a faith-based encounter with Jesus the Christ, the Son of the living God. The *Christ* quality also involves encounters and experiences with unchurched persons who claim a Christian spiritual journey, but are not regularly part of a Christ-centered, faith-based community. A subset of the unchurched is the underchurched, colloquially known as Chreasters; those who attend a congregation on Christmas and Easter plus a few scattered times during the year. Further, it involves encounters and experiences with dechurched persons who have been turned off by church and left it.

Congregation

Congregation is connecting people with a Christ-centered, faith-based community. This may involve ongoing participation with a local congregation, and even joining a congregation and accepting membership in a new or renewed commitment. This involves the subject areas of new membership recruitment and the initial assimilation of people into a local congregation, but not always in that order. It is about reaching out to potential new members or new people to connect with the congregation. It reflects the classic church growth categories of conversation, biological, and transfer growth.

Community

Community is more fully connecting people within a congregation, thus completing assimilation, or the process of assimilating new members into the full fellowship and care ministry components of the congregation. This is where the congregation with which people have chosen to connect truly becomes home. Their Relationships with people connected with the congregation have gone from face familiarity of a lot of people, to meaningful fellowship with a network of people, to deep friendships with people from at least six households. The deep friendships include people you can call at 3:00 a.m. if you need them, and in whose homes you have refrigerator rights.

Calling

It is essential in a disciplemaking process for people to engage in spiritual development and leadership development. This is the essence of *Calling*. It is where people connect with their spiritual giftedness, life skills, and personality preferences to continually prepare themselves for Christ-like service. This is a great contrast with the next quality— Programmatic Experiences. Calling at best focuses on the individual. Programs tend to focus on the masses. Calling addresses missional formation.

Commission

Lay mobilization is a key outcome, impact, and desired next aspect of the disciplemaking process. It is in mobilizing people as they are connected with the *Commission*. The implication is that people are connected with the Great Commission and Great Commandment as they discern, discover, develop, and act on their personal ministry *Calling*. They hold both Matthew 28:19-20 and Luke 4:18-19 in highest regard. It is also the missional engagement emphasis of Relationship Experiences.

Summary of Five C's

Relationship Experiences is the real thing. It is the style of disciplemaking for the congregation. It is the flavoring or identity of the congregation, while Visionary Leadership is the fuel or driving force for the congregation. The process of Relationship Experiences is dynamic and often organic. As such it does not necessarily occur in a linear manner as presented here, but is a process that can be entered at any one of these described places, and move in a chaordic pattern from one to another. [Chaordic is the simultaneous existence of chaos and order.]

Therefore, this system has five entry points into the Christian journey. People may enter in the *Commission* stage as they in some missional activity with a congregation with whom they are not directly connected. People may enter in the *Calling* stage by participating in some spiritual or leadership seminar offered by a congregation. Another entry point could be a seasonal worship experience or special event at a congregation. Therefore, it is important to highlight the value of Relationships at all times.

Relationships is about Being Missional

Relationship Experiences is where the missional nature of congregations is expressed. What does it take to be legitimately called a missional congregation? Not to co-opt the name and claim that is who you are, but to truly become a missional congregation. As a popular name or designation in many places, missional as a word and concept is being watered down.

First, let's start with a definition. Another one won't hurt, and it will also define the frame of these musings. A missional congregation is one who, out of their worship of the Triune God and their passion around fulfilling the Great Commission in the spirit of the Great Commandment, seeks to make the world more loving and just through actions focused on spiritually transforming the lives of their neighbors and modeling the gathering of these neighbors into healthy mission outposts called congregations for the scattering of these same neighbors through their own missional efforts. [Wow! That's a mouthful. Let's try a shorter version.]

A missional congregation is captivated by the *Missio Dei* meaning the mission of God, and seeks to make the world more loving and just through spiritually transforming the lives of neighbors.

Neighbors are defined here in a full global and local context. It is not a geographical neighbor but a theological neighbor. It is not neighbors to be attracted, but neighbors with whom we can represent the incarnational presence of the Triune God.

Missional congregations, while deeply caring for the needs within their congregation, are externally focused and seek to mobilize their congregation to be received, accepted, caught, embraced, and trusted by their neighbors. Missional congregations do not send missionaries and volunteers into their immediate or world context. Rather they invite people to be received by the neighbors for whom God has given them great passion. To be missional is more than to be sent. It is to be received by the people to whom you feel sent. To be genuine. To be internal agents within their culture. To present the gospel in contextually relevant ways. To share the gospel with people who are becoming our friends.

Since many congregations claim the term missional for what they do, let's break the concept down into three different types. First, *push missional* congregations are seeking to increase disciplemaking processes in their congregation to prepare people to go out into the mission field and express their gifts and passions to or at their neighbors. The desire may be to remake neighbors in the image of the sending congregations. I suspect it is the approach taken by 80 percent of congregations claiming to be missional. That is just a hunch. I have no research to support it.

Second, *pull missional* congregations are seeking to understand the neighbors to whom they perceive God has called them, and then equip disciples within their congregation with the skills and preferences needed to be received by those neighbors. The focus is on the receiving by the neighbors rather than the sending by the congregation. The desire is to remake neighbors in God's image instead of the image of the sending congregation. The Apostle Paul focused on this in seeking to be all things to all people that he might win some.

Third, *leap missional* congregations are seeking to connect with emerging cultures that often cannot be geographically defined, and for whom there are few if any people fully prepared to reach. These are cutting edge target groups composed of neighbors who may feel disenfranchised by God and the Church, or may have a clear awareness of neither. The desire is for neighbors to share back with us what the image of the Triune God ultimately looks like in their context, once they know the God who in Christ is reconciling the world. Congregations must re-image the stories of the gospel in a manner that speaks into the culture of the people while maintaining the truth of the gospel message.

Push is primarily boxed. *Pull* is moving beyond the box. *Leap* is outside the box and has declared it irrelevant. If your congregation is seeking to become missional, it must at least be *pull* in its focus. Anything less is not yet missional. Anything less is simply doing good to make you feel good. Anything less is a project rather than a lifestyle. Anything less is organizational rather than incarnational.

Importance of Relationship Experiences

The last generation of the 20th century focused on Visionary Leadership as the most important of the four *FaithSoaring* qualities. It remains the most important quality by which a congregation can be captivated. Often it is not the first thing a congregation must address in pursing *FaithSoaring*. It is probable that Relationship Experiences is the most important quality of the first generation of the 21st century. Why? As you review the several reasons below, keep in mind that Relationships Experiences are about relationships with God, one another, and the context in which we serve. The importance of these Relationships cannot be overstated, so let's emphasize it once more with these three points.

1. Spirituality is a key experience for many people; perhaps an increasingly significant experience for many. It is very personal. It is very popular. People desire to be part of a fellowship of believers and followers who are deeply related to the Triune God, and growing in that relationship. While they like Programs that are excellent, they do not want Programs devoid of meaning and substance. Time is the most precious commodity of the 21st century, and they want Relationship Experiences that are worth their time. This often means ones that clarify and deepen their spirituality.

    Architecturally, spiritually is symbolized by the sanctuary or worship space, and symbols within that space such as a cross, the altar, the communion table, stained-glass windows, and many other items. It can also be represented by a prayer room or a labyrinth as part of the facilities and grounds.

2. Friends are very important to many people. It may be friends you can call at 3:00 a.m. if you need them and they will not think you are crazy or put you off, or friends in whose homes you have refrigerator rights without asking. People do not just want a congregation where there is primarily face familiarity with people, or even meaningful fellowship with people connected with the congregation. They want deep friendships that propel church to the top of their list of time and effort priorities.

    An architectural symbol of the importance of these types of relationships is the increasing popularity of gathering spaces in church facilities. Once architects in designing the master plan for a congregation would begin with the sanctuary or worship space on the schematic, and then orient the rest of the facilities around it. Now they place the gathering space first, and organize everything else around it. Gathering space is the key place of relationships.

3. Causes are very important during this first generation of the 21st century. People want something in which they can believe and to which they can give their passion. They want to be part of a congregation that is on a journey that allows them to plug in missionally to the needs of a hurting world. In helping others many people work out their own hurts.

    A missional focus is probably not represented by any architectural symbol within church facilities. That is good. Missional should be represented by the community context or images of the target or affinity groups who are the focus of missional action. Perhaps Starbucks is one symbol of gathering in the context for relationships, with friends, to talk about causes. What are other such gathering places where causes can be enhanced?

Coaching Insights for Chapter Five

Personal Reflections for Learners

What is the strength of the Relationships quality in your congregation?

Consider and describe how Christ, Congregation, Community, Calling and Commission are being expressed in your congregation.

How is spirituality being cultivated on a person-to-person basis in your congregation?

How are people helped to intentionally move from face familiarity, to meaningful friendships, to deep friendships in your congregation?

What causes are encouraged and supported by your congregation? How missionally focused are these causes?

Your Reflections: **What are your reflections on the material presented in this chapters?**

Your Actions: **What actions do you need to take about your life, ministry, and/or congregation based on the material presented in this chapters?**

Your Accountability: **How and by whom do you want to be held accountable for taking these actions?**

Interlude

FaithSoaring is About Anticipating the Future

I will readily admit ice hockey is not my favorite sport. I have never been able to get into it. It reminds me of a roller derby on ice—if you are old enough to remember that sport which originated around 1935. Roller derby is a full contact sport. So are ice hockey and football. Basketball did not used to be a full contact sport, but it is becoming that way.

Well, now back to ice hockey. One of the greatest ice hockey players in history is Wayne Gretzky. He is credited with saying something like the following about his success in playing ice hockey: "Don't skate to where the hockey puck has been; skate to where it is going to be." It is possible this statement is an urban legend. No matter. It is still a statement that ought to make you think.

Whether Wayne or his father Walter said this is under debate. Whether this is good or bad advice for a hockey player is a matter of opinion. The point, however, is this might be a great strategic statement.

How can this be applied to the work of *FaithSoaring* Churches? Many ways. One example is that often when churches build a new building or renovate an existing one, they seek to correct their past to present space problems. Wise churches build for the type of space they will need 10 to 12 years from now.

At times, following a conflict, congregations will call a new pastor based on what they did not like about the last one they want to correct in the next one. Wise congregations build new capacity to handle diversity and health. Foolish congregations set themselves up to become repeat offenders in terms of unhealthy conflict.

FaithSoaring Churches anticipate the future rather than correct the past. It is much more prophetic to build a building for people you do not know yet, and to call a new pastor for a ministry you cannot characterize yet. All the time you know God is in the lead.

CHAPTER SIX

The Mind of Programs

Only Trinity lacks strong programs. All the others—Summit Heights, Christ the King, Nesmith, Lake Avenue, Midtown, and First—have strong programs. In some congregational cases this is a good thing. In others it is not. Keep reading to discover what makes the difference.

The Programs Quality

Programs are about Programmatic Emphases. A statement that summarizes it is as follows: Our congregation has outstanding programs, ministries, and activities for which we are well known throughout our congregation and our geographic community or the target or affinity groups we serve. Our programs, ministries, and activities seem to be growing in numbers and quality. Our programs are meeting real, identified spiritual, social, and emotional needs of people.

Programs, ministries, and activities are the visible expression and framework through which we anticipate the best possible Relationship Experiences that can occur with God, with one another, and with the context in which our congregation serves. Programs are a means to the desired end results, not the end results themselves. Success in programs, ministries, and activities do not necessarily mean success in the church. Programs must deepen and enhance Relationships.

Programs are the mind quality in the synergy of Vision, Relationships, Programs, and Management. It is in the development and sustaining of high quality Programs that the best strategic thinking can be applied to *FaithSoaring* Churches. That is brilliance of mind in the partnership with heart, soul, mind, and strength.

Programs are the functional attempts to provide programs, ministries, services, activities, and training for people connected to the congregation by membership, fellowship, or other relationship processes. Programs require planning, scheduling, budgeting, leadership recruitment, materials and equipment resources, implementation, and evaluation.

We can hold the evidence of Programs in our hands. It may be an event calendar, an activities budget, a strategic or program plan, a curriculum piece, enrollment and attendance reports, or evaluation sheets. We determine to do certain Programs in a congregation, plan for them, provide resources for them, prepare for them, conduct them, evaluate them, and then often do them all over again.

Programs, ministries, services, activities, and training include, but are not limited to: worship, music, education and training, age group programs such as youth/student ministry, and weekday and community ministries. Programs are focused on bringing new people into the congregation, or developing those who are connected. They are task oriented. Specific, concrete projects that the congregation engages in, such as building programs, are examples of projects that fit the broader category of programs.

The Weight of Programs

In some congregations it appears that Programs are the lead factor. They never are. But they can seem like they are because there are so many of them, they are so visible, and they are what are always being announced through various means. Programs are always a supporting factor and never a fueling factor.

Too many congregations seek to engage in too many Programs. The weight of a full load of Programs, and the percentage of time and leadership resources used to make Programs successful, can become a drag on a congregation rather than part of its soaring.

One of the writers, speakers, and consultants I have respected and followed for more than 30 years, Kennon Callahan, often says that congregations ought to plan to accomplish more by planning to do less. This would obviously be different from planning to accomplish less by planning to do more. What is meant is that congregations plan so many programs, they cannot do many, if any, of them with excellence that involves great preparation, great delivery, great follow-up, and great evaluation so the congregation knows how to improve them the next time.

One trap congregations get into is seeking to respond to the desire of its current or potential participants to offer programming for all age/stage groups from birth to death. This is an impossible task for well over 90 percent of all congregations. While a large number realize this is impossible to do, an equally large number keep trying to do it.

Here is my perspective. Back during the 1950s when life was simpler, there were around eight different and distinct life age/stage target groups of people on whom a congregation could theoretically focus. Now that number has grown to 16 with the increase in the life expectancy, and the diversification of the makeup or demographics of households.

For example, in the 1950s congregations had at most two categories of senior adult ministry. There were active, self-sufficient senior adults, and inactive, dependent senior adults. Now there are four categories of senior adults: active and still working full-time; active and semi-retired to retired; inactive but living in their homes and primarily independent; and inactive, dependent, and perhaps in a group or institutional living situation.

Another example is singles. Many congregations in the 1950s had little or no focus on single adults. That was not supposed to happen in a culture that focused on the nuclear family. Singles were at times marginalized. Today there are multiple foci on singles or singles in a new relationship. They include but are not limited to the following: young singles; divorced singles; widowed singles; mid-life singles; senior adult singles; singles now in a new marriage (perhaps with blended families); same gender unmarried couples; and cohabitating singles.

The proliferation of programs in congregations is also impacted by the number of birth generations present in a congregation. During the 1950s the typical congregation had three birth generations represented in the people connected with the congregation. Now many congregations have five birth generations and some are projecting programmatic needs for a sixth birth generation. All of the complicated Programs increase their weight on the right side of the metaphorical Lexus SUV.

Congregations need to resist the trap to try to have Programs for everyone. To illustrate this let me indicate what I think is happening in terms of critical mass of congregational participants and the number of Programs present in congregations. Question: How many people in average attendance does a congregation need to have first quality programs, ministries, services, and activities for all 16 primary age/stage target groups from birth to death?

Answer: In the 1950s they needed 400, in the 1960s 500, in the 1970s 600, in the 1980s 700, in the 1990s 800, in the 2000s 900, and in the current decade 1,000. That means that any congregation with less than 1,000 in average weekly worship attendance has to make choices about the Programs they initiate and sustain. Congregations must make choices or crumble under the weight of Programs.

Relationships vs. Programs

The end result differentiates Programs and Relationships. If the desired result is the ministry, activity, service, or training itself, then these elements act like Programs. Programs carried out in this manner can become the desired end result or goal themselves. The success of the Programs becomes the measurement of success for the congregation. It is output. It misses impact, capacity building, and sustainability.

However, Programs operated with a dynamic, flexible, process-orientation might be Relationship Experiences. The desired end result or goal is changed spiritual behavior as a result of the event or activity. The measurement of success is the development of the individual believer or disciple, or even of the preChristian.

Programs are task-oriented and provide stability for a congregation. Relationships Experiences are people-oriented and empower flexibility within a congregation. Programs are things congregations do or carry out. Relationships activities are things felt or experienced. For example, many congregations conduct Sunday School classes or other types of small groups. If in the midst of these classes new insight into Scripture is discovered, or if God is truly experienced as Lord in worship, then enhanced Relationships occurs. These activities remain Programs if the focus of Sunday School and worship is the habit, pattern, or doing of what is culturally acceptable in a particular congregation, or is only about growth in numbers.

A crucial issue is whether the events and experiences in your congregation are Programmatic Emphases, or Relationship Experiences. Let's use your primary worship experience as an example. If people leave worship services in your congregation primarily talking about having been to an event or met an obligation, liking or disliking it, feeling like they may come again next Sunday if they are in town and want to attend worship, then worship services in your congregation for these persons are a Programmatic Emphasis.

If people leave worship services in your congregation primarily talking about how great the experience was, how they felt the presence of God, how they were moved by the music and message, then worship services in your congregation for these people are Relationship Experiences.

Long-term congregational vitality and effectiveness are dependent on the ability to focus on creating and nurturing Relationship Experiences built on a foundation of Programmatic Emphases. Does that mean congregations should eliminate their Programmatic Emphases? No! Programmatic Emphases are a vital and crucial part of the organizing principles of congregations. Every congregation needs a strategy, structure, and system for Programmatic Emphases.

What it means is that congregations must have Programmatic Emphases and Relationship Experiences in proper alignment with one another. The purpose of Programmatic Emphases should be to enable genuine Relationship Experiences to take place in the lives of individuals, groups within the congregation, and the congregation as a whole.

When congregations focus on the Vision of God that is shared within their fellowship, then the focus given to Programmatic Emphases moves to a focus on people. Therefore, Programmatic Emphases that are dynamic, flexible, and fuel the Relationship Experiences will also fuel the future direction of the congregation.

Programs focus on numbers and Relationships focuses on names. *FaithSoaring* Churches focus on names more than they focus on numbers. Try this experiment. Let's say that your congregation goes through a season when attendance is down. If the focus of your congregation is Programs success then the concern will be about how numbers are down. If the focus of your congregation is on deepening Relationships, then it will be important to discover who is not in attendance and what might be going on in their lives that needs to be pursued by God's people.

FaithSoaring Churches identify the households who miss three Sundays in a row. They then contact them to be sure everything is all right. Often these people have experienced a life event that has altered their congregational participation, or have had an incident related to the congregation that needs clarifying. Other congregations are not concerned until people have missed a month or two. What they do not realize is that once people miss two or more months, they may have already left the congregation or decided to leave by some future date.

The Role of Management in Programs

When Management is the lead quality among Vision, Relationships, Programs, and Management, it has a definite impact on Programs. When congregations focus on Management as the lead element, the emphasis on Relationship Experiences moves to an emphasis on maintaining Programmatic Emphases. Congregations who focus on maintaining long-term and less effective Programmatic Emphases, particularly if they focus primarily on long-term members, will have difficulty sustaining a broad-based ownership of God's Vision for the congregation. Because Management takes over when Vision diminishes, then Programs, rather than Relationships, become the desired outward sign of success.

In reality there is a co-dependent relationship between Programs and Management. To engage in Programs it is necessary to have space, finances, materials, and staff. Management provides all of this. Because management enjoys providing these, it also supports the premise that more Programs are automatically needed when actually in order to be *FaithSoaring,* more Vision and Relationships are needed.

Therefore, inherently, Programs and Management will work against congregations being *FaithSoaring* Churches. Sad, but true.

Coaching Insights for Chapter Six

Personal Reflections for Learners

What are the types of Programs in your congregation, and the people groups on which they focus?

What are some of the programs, ministries, services, and activities for which your congregation is best known?

In what ways do your Programs support and undergird the development of deep Relationships with God, one another, and the context in which you serve?

In what ways are Programs the output the congregation is seeking, rather than a means to the impact your congregation needs?

Your Reflections: **What are your reflections on the material presented in this chapter?**

Your Actions: **What actions do you need to take about your life, ministry, and/or congregation based on the material presented in this chapter?**

Your Accountability: **How and by whom do you want to be held accountable for taking these actions?**

Interlude

It's the Big Things, Pilgrim

FaithSoaring is about the big things, not the small things. It is about the things that really matter, not the things about which only a few people care. It is about the things that empower, not the things that control. It is about the new, narrow road, and not the wide, beaten path.

FaithSoaring Church is about worship that provides a genuine encounter with the Triune God that refreshes, restores, and renews relationships with God, one another and the context in which we serve. *FaithSoaring* Church is about discipleship development that invites, involves, and inspires followers of Jesus as they seek to "grow in the grace and knowledge of our Lord and Savior, Jesus Christ" [2 Peter 3:18, NASB].

FaithSoaring Church is about caring relationships that encourage, create enthusiasm, evolve into deep, meaningful relationships over the years and embrace members, regular attendees, guests, and seekers into a fellowship that recognizes everyone as a person of worth created in the image of God to live and to love.

FaithSoaring Church is not about the color of the walls in the education building, the regulation of the temperature in classrooms, who should be punished for breaking the street light outside the gym during the student fellowship, or paying more on the debt this year rather than reaching missions funding goals.

What are the big things on which your church places its greatest focus? What are the small things that keep pushing up like weeds to smother your view of the big things? What does your church need to do to sharpen its focus on the big things, and ignore the small things? In the spirit of John Wayne, it's the big things, pilgrim.

CHAPTER SEVEN

The Strength of Management

Only Lake Avenue and Midtown lack strong Management. In both of their cases this is a good thing. In Summit Heights and Nesmith it is definitely a good thing that they have strong Management. In Christ the King, Trinity, and First it is not a good thing that they have strong Management. In these three congregations Management has reached a point that it diminishes the quality of congregation life rather than enhances it. How can this be?

The Management Quality

Management is about Accountable Management. A statement that summarizes it is as follows: Our congregation has excellent, flexible management systems that empower the future direction of our congregation rather than seeking to control the future direction. Decision-making is open and responsive to congregational input. Finances are healthy and increasing each year. The management systems are supportive of the Visionary Leadership efforts by the pastor, staff, and congregational leadership.

Depending on the polity of your congregation, management groups could be teams, committees, councils, boards, leadership communities, sessions, vestries, or commissions. These are the strength characteristic in the partnership of heart, soul, mind, and strength. It is a very important part of the synergy of Vision, Relationships, Programs, and Management, but nevertheless a support role. At the same time the people of these management groups have the greatest potential to control congregations rather than empowering them. In many congregations, their capacity to control is stronger than the capacity of Visionary Leadership to empower.

Management is the administration of the various resources of the congregation, the formal and informal governance and decision-making structure of the congregation, the formal and informal traditions and culture of the congregation, and the readiness of the congregation for change and growth.

Management also relates to how a congregation handles its day-to-day operations. This includes its operational planning process and how this is implemented to bring about growth and change in the congregation. This quality provides a basis for deciding how the people, finances, facilities, and equipment and material resources of the congregation are utilized.

Management deals with the efficiency of a congregation. Once a congregation attains the stage of Maturity on the congregational life cycle, its progress tends to be fueled by Management rather than Vision. Over a number of years, these management principles become increasingly controlling. Ultimately Management becomes dysfunctional and management principles begin to break down.

Management may be observed through five lenses: resources, governance, transition and culture, readiness for transition and change, and operations.

Resources

The definition of resources needs to be expanded in the typical congregation. Too often congregations think only about money. The resources of a congregation are people and things. "People" include the pastor, staff, and lay leadership. Thus management relates to the process of calling a pastor or other staff ministers. The infrastructure that mobilizes laity is included here. Lay mobilization as a movement is part of relationships.

"Things" include the finances, the facilities, the equipment, and various materials. These things are not intended to be in a lead role in the life of a congregation. They are intended to be resources that help the congregation fulfill its Vision by empowering Relationships. Many congregations have this reversed. *FaithSoaring* Churches have these things in a healthy alignment or synergy.

Governance

Governance relates to the administration and decision-making structure of the congregation. This includes the formal committees, councils, and boards, as well as the process for making decisions. It also includes the governing documents. *FaithSoaring* Churches know that the longer and more detailed the governing documents, and the more careful it adheres to functioning within the governing documents, the less likely the congregation is to be *FaithSoaring.*

Governance and decision-making are intended to help guide or navigate the congregational processes, and to continually develop ownership within the congregation. Some congregations mistake governance and decision-making as the manner by which they are to control the congregation. Governance and decision-making should be as invisible as possible, and visible only as necessary to encourage deep ownership by the participants in the congregation.

Tradition and Culture

Management may seem like an odd place for tradition and culture. In reality they are commodities that congregations deposit like financial assets in a bank. Their tendency is to maintain more than to empower. Some congregations add elements of tradition and culture to the list of core values of the congregation and overload core values with things that are really negotiable.

The way things have been from the past is more accepted and wanted than the way things could be. The way things have been makes more people happy. The way things could be makes more people doubt, even fear, the journey. The past to present may be mediocre, and could even have been dysfunctional at points, yet it is the proven pathway. Proven or not, it is not the way of *FaithSoaring* Churches.

Readiness for Transition and Change

When management is handled in a flexible, supportive way, it helps congregations to be prepared for the new innovation or the new sense of God's movement. When management is used to control, it shuts down the readiness for change and transition in favor of maintaining the tradition and culture of the congregation. This is because change, even when for the better, is seen as loss.

The 20th century was about changing things. The 21st century is about transitioning people. Management is usually about changing things. If it could find a way to focus on transitioning people to the emerging realities, transitioning policies to the emerging reality, and transitioning governance groups to the emerging reality, then it would be bringing its best strengths to *FaithSoaring* Churches. The emerging reality revolves around supporting Visionary Leadership.

Operations

Operations describe the day-to-day activities and functions of the congregation. Operations should be first of all effective, and then efficient, in support of the future of the congregation. Efficiency often dominates effectiveness. This fits easily into the strengths characteristic of management. If you want great implementation, Accountable Management is the essential quality.

Day-to-day operations are typically carried out by the staff of the congregation. When too much of the day-to-day operations are carried out by lay volunteers, it could mean one of several things. First, the congregation is a smaller membership church where much of the overall operations are carried out by lay volunteers. Second, the congregation has a two career or bi-vocational pastor, and lay leaders must step up and take responsibility for significant parts of the operations. Third, the congregation is an economic position where it must rely more on volunteers than unpaid staff. All of these first three are typical, normal, and healthy.

Or, fourth, a distrustful relationship exists between the governance of the congregation, long-term members and participants in the congregation, and the staff of the congregation. Rather than freeing up and empowering the staff to lead the congregation, management volunteers feel the need to monitor and do for the congregation that which they feel like the staff is incapable of doing or is doing wrong. Being a *FaithSoaring* Church and having this approach to operations will never happen at the same time

Managing by Leadership Communities

FaithSoaring Churches are managed by leadership communities who have taken on administrative tasks as a sacred trust for the life and ministry of the congregation. They believe deeply and passionately that their work is to undergird and lift up the *FaithSoaring* nature of the congregation. They do this by being accountable to Visionary Leadership. In everything they do, they ask the question, "How is this going to help our congregation live into God's Vision for our future?" If any proposed action or decision does not support the God-given Vision of the congregation, unless there is absolutely no other alternative, they do not take that action or make that decision.

These leadership communities have no interest in demonstrating their own importance or how powerful they are. They glory in the ability to give away power to others. They want their congregation to soar with faith as a high percentage of the active congregation engages in the Programs and Relationships of the congregation.

To the extent the polity of their denominational family will allow, these leadership communities seek to develop a distributed or networked approach to leadership and management in the life and ministry of their congregation. They are always encouraging informality in task and relationship-oriented groups, and place few restrictions on emerging programs, ministries, services, and activities except that they focus on vision fulfillment.

The traditional management systems are often referred to as a box which contains the things that are allowed. These leadership communities see the core values, and the lean and mean essential rules and regulations of the congregation, as being in the center or the middle of the congregation. Innovation is given as much freedom, and lack of boundaries as possible so that as the Triune God leads, the congregation and its various networks might be *FaithSoaring.*

Managing by Executive Committees

Some congregational management patterns call for a formal or intentional executive committee. Some congregational management patterns result in an informal or unintentional executive committee. The formal executive committees go by such names as boards, councils, sessions, committees, vestries, and others. They are formally required by the governing documents of the congregation. They have great potential for help and can be an instrument of creativity for *FaithSoaring* Churches.

Simultaneously, they have great potential for hurt and can be an instrument of control which prevents congregations from ever being *FaithSoaring* Churches. The choice is theirs. At times it is not the governing documents which are the problem. It is the personality or perspective of the participants on the executive committee. It is the dimension of spirituality which they bring to their work. It is their dependency on the past for stability. It is their self-esteem about their own life work. It is the health of their personal and family life. It is their emotional maturity. It is the strengths or skills which they bring to their work.

Informal or unintentional executive committees sometimes arise within congregations. This happens regardless of whether or not there is a formal or intentional executive committee already in place. This is typically a group of people who think they know best for the congregation. At times their motives are good. Their desire for their congregations to be *FaithSoaring* Churches is real. They just do not realize that their actions control their congregation rather than empower their congregation. They have a support group that nudge them forward in their actions to do the right things.

In many congregations, the members of this informal or unintentional executive committee are very well known. The rumor mill or grapevine in the congregation says that it's always these same five or six people who seek to control everything. In some congregations this group of people is unknown or secretive. Periodically I've encountered some of these underground groups. I have even been present in congregations when they called the pastor in to give him/her their orders or instructions as to what to do next. Almost never does this style allow congregations to be *FaithSoaring* Churches.

The Management Focus

In too many congregations the focus on management is on things that do not contribute to the spiritual and strategic strength of management. The focus is not on empowerment, but on control. The focus is not on leaning into the future, but falling into the past. The focus is not on new ways of managing, but old ways that may or may not serve the congregation well. To be a *FaithSoaring* Church the management practices must be empowering, future-oriented, and continually considering new ways of engaging in sound management practices. At the same time, the management systems must be sound, moral, ethical, legal, and filled with grace rather than judgment.

Three things are very important for the management systems in a congregation to keep in mind:

1. Management must always be innovative rather than allocative. It must always be looking for ways to do new things in new ways with new people led by inspired and imaginative leaders. It must be looking for choices to take on challenges that stretch the congregation beyond where it has been.

Take the church budget as an example. When congregations face financial crises, where budget expenditures are out of whack, they often want to think about their budget as a pie. When the way the pie is currently sliced is no longer working, they want to allocate the pie in different ways focused on what is defined as fixed costs.

Seldom are missional engagements seen as fixed costs. Usually facilities costs are at the top of the list. Second are personnel costs. Third are programs, ministries, services, and activities. Last are missional engagements. Initially the pie is re-allocated to lessen missional engagement costs. Next programming is impacted. Once a congregation gets to cutting personnel they are in serious trouble.

A much better approach would be to declare the congregation needs a different kind of pie. Move from apple to pecan, or coconut to chocolate, or lemon to key lime. Address the multiple funding streams of the congregation, and the financial stewardship commitment or generosity of the people connected with the congregation. Find new funding streams before cutting into the center of the pie. Avoid the cut back syndrome in areas critical to the overall mission and Vision of the congregation.

2. Management must recognize that congregations are not in their heart, soul, mind, nor strength for-profit business organizations. They are nonprofit spiritual organisms, and as such secular management principles will only go so far in helping congregations become *FaithSoaring* Churches.

    In many congregations, the people who are placed on management groups are often people who speak out of a gospel of Matthew, or even an Old Testament perspective, judging the rightness of management practices rather than the goodness. Their intentions are honorable. Their loyalty is deep. Their belief in the past and present of the congregation is commendable.

    At the same time I can often walk into a meeting of a financial administrative group in a congregation, and within five minutes know that our primary conversations are going to be about tactical issues, or reshuffling the chairs on the Titanic. Sometimes I'm wrong. Sometimes people surprise me with a deep and warm heart for the grace-filled ministry of the congregation and the kingdom of God.

    One sign is how quickly they want to pull out the church's constitution and bylaws, a book of order, or a book of discipline. When a congregation faces a tremendous opportunity or challenge, the legal, bureaucratic, or ecclesiastical documents are seldom empowering of the next steps. They certainly may keep the congregation from falling, but they do not provide the joy of walking the wire, as in The Wallenda Factor which was described in an early Interlude in this book.

3. Management must never believe it can administrate the congregation into having Vision. That would be a push approach and will not work. Vision is a pull approach, with God doing the pulling. Too many management people believe they can will the church forward into success. They totally misunderstand that it is the will of God that matters. This is another place where the wisdom of Kennon Callahan comes into play. I used to hear Kennon talk about the fact that you can fix everything that's wrong with the church and bring it right up to neutral. Fixing everything that's wrong will not propel a church forward, or allow it to be pulled forward. It is what's right, good, loving, and strong about the church that will enable it to be pulled forward by God into the future.

Vision is about God-like solutions, and not human-like fixes. A congregation can fix the budget, fix the buildings, fix the decision-making processes, fix the staff accountability system, fix the day-to day operations, fix the pastor by getting a new one, fix the denomination by leaving it, fix the programs, and a multitude of other things, and still not bring forth a solution that will allow the congregation to leap forward as a *FaithSoaring* Church.

A Closing Word

One easy, yet not at every point respectful, way to remember what Accountable Management refers to is to remember the words, *Bodies, Bucks, Boards,* and *Buildings. Bodies* refer to the people who are called or appointed, employed, or who volunteer in the life of the congregation. *Bucks* refer to the finances of the congregation. Informal and formal decision-making processes are the *Boards. Buildings* apply to both facilities and capital equipment.

Coaching Insights for Chapter Seven

Personal Reflections for Learners

Describe the strength and manner of Management in your congregation.

In what ways is Accountable Management in your congregation controlling and in what ways is it empowering of Visionary Leadership?

Characterize resources, governance, tradition and culture, readiness for transition and change, and operations in your congregation.

Too many congregations are over managed and under led. To be a *FaithSoaring* Church there must be a proper balance with Vision in the lead role and Management in a supporting role. How is your congregation doing?

Your Reflections: **What are your reflections on the material presented in this chapter?**

Your Actions: **What actions do you need to take about your life, ministry, and/or congregation based on the material presented in this chapter?**

Your Accountability: **How and by whom do you want to be held accountable for taking these actions?**

Interlude

Trusting the Holy Spirit

Is the Holy Spirit trustworthy? Hang on. This is not a blasphemous question. The obvious answer is "yes." Perhaps the real question we ought to be asking is, "Does our church act like we believe the Holy Spirit is trustworthy?"

FaithSoaring is about trusting the Holy Spirit. This probably sounds like a simple, core commitment for Christians. If so, why is it so hard for so many congregations? Trusting the Holy Spirit requires your willingness to surrender to the movement of the Holy Spirit within the life and ministry of your church. Some church leaders feel they must hold the reins of control to be sure the outcome is what they want. They want their church to be remade in their image rather than God's image.

What does a FaithSoaring Church that trusts the Holy Spirit look like? It focuses on discernment. It focuses on empowering people to live out of their sense of spiritual giftedness, life skills and personality preferences. It focuses on its spiritual strategic direction. It is not anxious. It knows God is at work in everyone, and we need to get busy about serving Him. It takes leaps of faith into uncharted territories with the assurance the Holy Spirit is alongside and leading.

What does a non-FaithSoaring Church that does not trust the Holy Spirit look like? Such a church makes cultural decisions more often than spiritual decisions. It focuses on controlling people, and assigning those tasks. It trusts only in the things it can see and touch. It focuses on programmatic responses to perceived needs. It backs away from opportunities to make significant Kingdom progress because it is more concerned about what it may lose than what it may gain.

CHAPTER EIGHT

FaithSoaring Synergy

Of the seven congregations, only Summit Heights has a full synergy of Vision, Relationships, Programs, and Management. I have previously stated that Summit Heights and Nesmith are *FaithSoaring* Churches. That remains true. However, Nesmith currently does not have a full synergy of the four qualities. It is missing a fully captivating Vision. Christ the King, Lake Avenue, Trinity, and First are missing two of the four qualities.

Midtown has not been in existence long enough to qualify as a *FaithSoaring* Church. If it stays open and innovative, it is likely to be a *FaithSoaring* Church at some point in the future. It is important that it continue developing in the positive ways it has been experiencing, and that it not institutionalize when it reaches the end of its first generation of life.

Nesmith could achieve full synergy again in a year or two if it re-envisions its future. Lake Avenue is also headed in the right direction. Within five to seven years, if it redevelops Management as an empowering quality, it will be there. Christ the King, Trinity, and First have some serious issues to address before they would be considered *FaithSoaring* Churches.

What is *FaithSoaring* Synergy?

Let's review what we have said earlier. Synergy occurs when multiple qualities work together to achieve a result that is geometrically greater than the result that any one of them could have achieved independently. In the case of *FaithSoaring* Churches these qualities are Vision, Relationships, Programs, and Management. No one of these qualities, as good as they are, can enable a congregation to soar with faith. It takes a synergy of all four for *FaithSoaring* to be achieved.

FaithSoaring Churches are captivated by the optimal synergy or interplay of Vision, Relationships, Programs, and Management. Without this synergy there is no *FaithSoaring*.

The reality is that this ideal configuration that produces synergy is elusive for congregations. It is difficult to achieve. Once achieved it does not usually last more than seven to nine years without intentional action to rebalance Vision, Relationships, Programs, and Management. Without rebalancing, they will be out of balance; they will significantly and negatively impact the journey of a congregation

Using the image of a Lexus SUV with Vision, Relationships, Programs, and Management as the passengers, let's look at the ten stages of the life cycle of a congregation and when synergy occurs with them. You will want to study the congregational life cycle chart at the end of this chapter.

The Journey to Achieve Synergy

Birth: When a congregation is founded, Vision is driving. Relationships, Programs, and Management are asleep in the back seat. Their roles are not yet needed as distinctive qualities in the journey. The congregation is accelerating from zero to 60 as fast as it can with Vision behind the wheel. Relationships, Programs, and Management are expressed out of the overflow of the euphoria surrounding Vision. In the life cycle of a congregation this is the Birth stage, and it will last six months to two years.

This is good, but *FaithSoaring* has not yet been achieved.

Infancy: Vision gets to the point that it needs the assistance of formalized or systematic Relationships to take the congregation to the next stage of development. It reaches back and wakes up Relationships, who joins Vision in the front seat. Forward progress has been fueled and achieved by Vision alone. Now navigation and flavoring, or increasing the quality of the journey, is needed. Relationships are the right quality to handle that. Deep Relationships are now the focus so that Relationships with God, one another, and the context in which the congregation serves can add breadth and depth to the journey. Let's call this stage Infancy.

This is good, but *FaithSoaring* has not yet been achieved.

Childhood: After Vision has been driving for five to six years it becomes obvious the journey is going to be a lasting and enduring one. While excitement around Vision fulfillment is high, and the quality of Relationships is outstanding, the congregation reaches a place where a Programmatic framework is needed to sustain the Relationships movement.

Vision asks Relationships to wake up Programs, and then switch places to allow Programs to navigate for a while, and promises that Relationships will get to sit in the front seat again soon. As the formal Programmatic Emphases framework is being developed, Vision wants Programs near it so it can be sure Programs thoroughly understand Vision. For the next five to six years, in a stage known as Childhood, a Programmatic Emphases framework is developed that will sustain for the whole rest of the first generation of the congregation.

This is good, but *FaithSoaring* has not yet been achieved.

In some congregations, as their journey takes them through Childhood, Vision all of a sudden realizes that it made a mistake by allowing Programs to navigate. It misses the high touch of Relationships. Programs are taking the congregation a direction in its journey Vision did not intend. It this feeling lingers too long, Vision will abort the journey, wake up Management and turn the driving over to it. Worn out from the journey, Vision moves into the back seat to take a nap. When this happens, Management is prematurely driving and only knows to take the congregation directly to a Retirement mindset, and skip the joy of the remainder of the journey. In this case *FaithSoaring* is never achieved.

Adolescence: Childhood ended up being an overbearing stage where Vision and Programs tire themselves out seeking to form the Programs framework. Vision finally calls a stop to this lunacy and asks Programs to move back to the back seat, and allow Relationships to navigate once again. However, Programs is to stay awake and continually figure out how it can support Relationships.

This is Adolescence, which is a stage when Vision is driving, Relationships are navigating, Programs are in the back seat supporting Relationships, and Management is still asleep. It tends to last about six to eight years.

Does this mean the congregation is not being managed? No. It means the Management systems are not yet fully developed and integrated into the culture of the congregation. At most, in some denominations, Management is what a guide or discipleship book from the denomination dictates, rather than the unique system that has been developed within a congregation.

Adolescence is a chaordic time in a congregation when both chaos and order are present. Vision is still strongly focused on the journey in response to God's call. It will not be deterred from moving forward. Relationships and Programs, who are intended to work together, are competing for the attention of Vision. Both of them like navigating.

One illustration of this is when a congregation needs to expand its facilities during Adolescence. People focused on Relationships, who likely connected with the congregation during Birth or Infancy, believe the next building ought to be a worship or sanctuary building symbolizing a deeper relationship with God, or a fellowship facility or gathering space symbolizing their relationship with one another.

People focused on Programs, who likely connected with the congregation during Childhood, believe the next building ought to be educational and recreation space for preschoolers, children, and youth. Both foci are positive. Both groups have deep passion about their perspective. Each facility would define the next phase of the congregation's ministry.

All the commotion of Adolescence finally wakes Management up, and it studies what is going on and then inserts itself into the journey. It feels the need to bring order to what is happening. Vision stays focused on making forward progress, and Management begins to be sure that everything is appropriately supporting Vision. It builds the administrative infrastructure that can best empower Vision.

This is good, but *FaithSoaring* has not yet been achieved.

The Journey to Sustain Synergy

Adulthood: About 18 to 22 years after the journey began, the congregation reaches the stage known as Adulthood. It is where Vision is driving, Relationships are navigating, and Programs and Management are providing a framework and infrastructure respectively. This is synergy. The congregation has achieved *FaithSoaring* status. They have many, if not all, of the characteristics mentioned in chapter three as those held by *FaithSoaring* Churches.

Vision, Relationships, Programs, and Management are no longer conforming to an outside set of guidelines or restrictions. They are not competing with one another for position and influence. They are collaborating to achieve synergy as a *FaithSoaring* Church. They are soaring with faith toward a destination that can only be seen with their heart, soul, mind, and strength.

This describes the situation of Summit Heights at 27 years since its founding, and as a congregation that had reached Adulthood 18 years after its Birth. Approximately four years ago it realized that was the best time to redream the dream of being a congregation. It re-envisioned and spiraled forward to a new and stronger Adulthood rather than proceeding forward to Maturity. It added affiliation to a national affinity group of *FaithSoaring* Churches to its connection with its denomination of heritage. It is truly a congregation that hums.

Maturity: When a congregation is about 22 to 27 years old, Vision wanes. It needs to take a nap in the back seat. It needs a respite; not a retirement. For the first time in its life Management is driving. In the Maturity stage this is a good thing. Someone needs to drive. Management, after Vision, is the next best quality to drive. It best understands what Vision has been doing and the skills it takes to drive.

Maturity is a very positive stage in the life of a congregation. The congregation may still have almost all of the characteristics of a *FaithSoaring* Church. One thing is for sure—Maturity can be the outstanding stage in the life of a congregation. Although Vision has diminished, Relationships as supported by Programs continues to soar. In a certain sense it feels like a more empowering stage in some congregations than was Adulthood. The congregation is doing great things. It just does not know why anymore. It has lost Vision.

Maturity fools congregations into thinking they are still soaring. One way to describe this is by considering the lyrics of the song "Fallin & Flyin" sung by Jeff Bridges in the movie *Crazy Heart*: "Funny how fallin' feels like flyin' for a little while."

Unlike Summit Heights as mentioned above, Nesmith chose to hang on during Adulthood believing they were on the right track and that their *FaithSoaring* nature would continue for years to come. It did not. Vision diminished and the Lexus SUV of Nesmith was running on fumes. The high quality stage of Maturity is still a good platform for Nesmith to renew its Vision and spiral forward to a new *FaithSoaring* status.

Sustaining: Sustaining is not a unique stage of a congregation's life cycle. It is the action that congregations must take if they are in Adulthood and Maturity and desire to redevelop forward. If *FaithSoaring* is the best place to be, why not stay there? It is a reasonable and expected thing for *FaithSoaring* Churches to wonder how they can sustain *FaithSoaring* rather than moving on to Maturity. It is inevitable that at some point once they achieve Adulthood, and enjoy it a while, that they will move forward to Maturity. God's world is a dynamic world. It is ever-changing. Nothing stays exactly the same.

After four to nine years as a *FaithSoaring* Church, virtually every congregation is going to move forward to Maturity. Once there it cannot go back. But, it can go forward. How? In fact, *FaithSoaring* Churches will go forward with an intentional side trip in their journey that brings them once again into Adulthood. *FaithSoaring* Churches who are sustaining experience a pattern of Adulthood, then Maturity, then a new Adulthood, and then a new Maturity, and so forth. They experience this full pattern about every decade.

This allows them to experience congregational life in a two-stage place called Prime. In Prime congregations must lose their status as a *FaithSoaring* Church so they can transform and move forward to a new experience of being a *FaithSoaring* Church. They gain by losing.

A decade or so ago Trinity missed several great opportunities to sustain its existence as a *FaithSoaring* Church. It reached Maturity, and then moved into a stance of denial about having lost Visionary Leadership, and now have their Lexus SUV being driven by Accountable Management. They never recovered from this denial and lost synergy and their *FaithSoaring* status, perhaps permanently.

Again, this is the opposite of Summit Heights who never denied their situation of moving from Adulthood to Maturity. Rather they saw it as the opportunity to envision a new life, a new journey, a new Vision from God. They truly are an example of the separation of the *FaithSoaring* from the non-*FaithSoaring*. Yet, the same opportunity was available to Trinity. They missed it.

The Journey When Synergy is Lost

Empty Nest: If a congregation does not redevelop forward during the Maturity stage, Programs begin to diminish. Their cutting edge nature and their attendance begin to diminish. The arrangement of the four qualities is that

Management is driving, Relationships are navigating, but now Programs are not only in the back seat, they are asleep along with Vision. To once again be a *FaithSoaring* Church is beyond simply re-envisioning their future. It now requires a diminishing of the now controlling aspects of Management, revitalizing Programs, and then casting new Vision.

Anger grows the longer a congregation is in Empty Nest. This anger symbolizes the loss of synergy and long-term thinking. Congregations begin to develop a greater sense of urgency. They work harder not smarter. They seek to push the congregation forward because they no longer have a Vision that drives them in the direction of God's pulling.

Retirement: If a congregation does not redevelop forward during the Empty Nest stage, then Relationships begin to diminish. Relationships turn inward within the congregation. Spiritual Relationships with the Triune God, and Relationships within the context in which the congregation serves start to weaken and become more distant.

The arrangement of the qualities is that Management continues to drive and solidify that role, Programs are now navigating. Relationships and Vision are asleep in the back seat. Programs reassert themselves not because of a proactive and positive strategy, but because the congregation at this stage wrongly feels the solution to their dilemma is Programs.

To once again be a *FaithSoaring* Church these congregations need to renew their Relationships with God, one another, and their context, followed by focusing on new Programmatic Emphases that emanate out of those new Relationships, and finally to cast new Vision.

Old Age: If a congregation does not redevelop forward during the Retirement stage, then Programs diminish again and nothing takes its place. No one is navigating. Vision, Relationships, and Programs are all three asleep in the back seat of the Lexus SUV. Only Management is awake and functioning. Therefore, it can do anything it wants to do without opposition.

To once again be a *FaithSoaring* Church these congregations must reinvent themselves. They must begin with a clean sheet of paper and redesign what they need to be at this time and in this place. They must engage in an Extreme Congregational Makeover. [See www.ExtremeCongregationalMakeover.info.]

Death: If a congregation does not spiral forward to a new partial life cycle during Old Age, they may eventually die. The Lexus SUV stops. It has run out of fuel, it has no sense of navigating toward any destination, and it has no support from the back seat. Yet, it is possible for a new congregation to be resurrected out of the ashes of the old congregation.

Interestingly the death of a congregation can be a tremendous opportunity to launch a new *FaithSoaring* Church. Actions following death are certainly reflective of an Extreme Congregational Makeover.

FaithSoaring Churches Have a Sunroof

The Lexus SUV, the symbol of the journey of a *FaithSoaring* Church, has a sunroof. The cover slides back easily, and it opens with the push of a button so all can see the wide expanse of God's universe. At least on days there is not a thick cloud cover.

FaithSoaring Churches have a wide view of ministry in God's kingdom. The roof of their car is not a solid ceiling that prohibits them from soaring in spirit and in reality. Because of this, they do not have to take detours due to one or more of the following reasons:

1. **Low Ceilings:** Non-*FaithSoaring* Churches, where Management has been in control way too long, have low ceilings. The possibilities for transition, change, and innovation they are willing to consider is a short list, and one where they control what goes on that list and what does not. A futurist friend of mine, Rick Smyre, once commented that "the most conservative thing the management of an organization can do is to change something. If they initiate the change and lead its implementation, then guess who is still in charge once the change occurs?"

   FaithSoaring Churches have no ceiling. They soar without unreasonable limits to the heights where God is leading them. Their journey is not perfect, so on some days they do have to make their way around clouds, and on a few days the solid cloud cover—also known in aviation tribes as a low ceiling—causes them to wait for God's perfect timing.

2. **Solid Ceilings:** Non-*FaithSoaring* Churches, where the 60-40-20 People believe they have preferred stock in the congregation, have heights beyond which they will not go because it disconnects them with the traditions and culture of the congregation as they see it. 60-40-20 People are people at least 60 years old, and at least 40 years a professing Christian, and at least 20 years a member of this congregation.

   They believe their ownership of the congregation makes it all right for them to control the congregation and to not allow it to soar with faith. They believe the principles and practices of the past to present will work if they work on them hard enough. Generally they see problems with what is happening with the congregation, and believe the Lexus SUV has veered from the proven path for the journey.

3. **Not Knowing Which Way is Up:** Non-*FaithSoaring* Churches cannot distinguish between staying busy and making progress. Because they are not driven by Vision, they do not know how to evaluate the rightness and goodness of their direction. *FaithSoaring* Churches can always see through the sunroof, if not straight ahead, that they are headed in the right direction.

4. **Stale Air:** Non-*FaithSoaring* Churches often follow the classic colloquial definition of insanity: doing the same thing over and over again and expecting different results. These congregations grow stale over the years by doing the same things, the same way, with the same leadership, and with the same diminishing results. At some point in the past the things they are doing were new, sharp, and effective. Either circumstances changed, the context changed, or what they had been doing simply became stale and no longer had an empowering impact.

   Faith-Soaring Churches simply open up the sunroof and let some fresh air in, without blowing everyone around, as would happen if they opened the windows. They are continually innovating the style of what they are doing, although they may be using the same or similar structures to address the same substance. The continual newness—known in industrial psychology as the Hawthorne effect—helps them to soar with faith.

The Life Cycle and Stages of Congregational Development

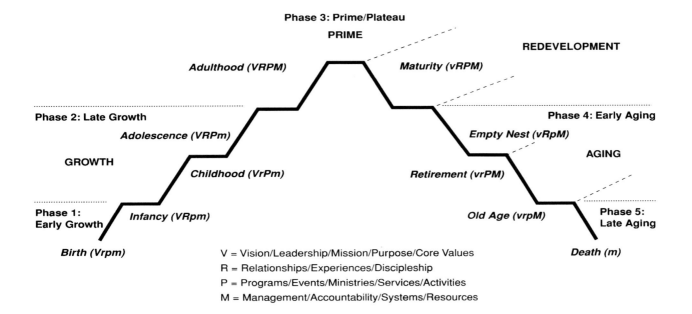

V = Vision/Leadership/Mission/Purpose/Core Values
R = Relationships/Experiences/Discipleship
P = Programs/Events/Ministries/Services/Activities
M = Management/Accountability/Systems/Resources

Copyright 2009, Rev. George Bullard, D.Min.
Provided by The Columbia Partnership at www.TheColumbiaPartnership.org. Contact at Client.Care@
TheColumbiaPartnership.org or 803.622.0923
[Consult George's book Pursuing the Full Kingdom Potential of Your Congregation.]

Coaching Insights for Chapter Eight

Personal Reflections for Learners

Describe the synergy, or lack thereof, in your congregation of Vision, Relationships, Programs, and Management.

Where is your congregation on the journey to achieve, sustain, or regain synergy? Describe what the journey currently looks like in your congregation.

What is the synergy of the essential elements in your Lexus SUV? Does it represent *FaithSoaring*? If not, what steps do you need to take to achieve synergy?

How is your congregation dealing with low ceilings, solid ceilings, not knowing which way is up, and stale air in your Lexus SUV with a sunroof?

Your Reflections: **What are your reflections on the material presented in this chapter?**

Your Actions: **What actions do you need to take about your life, ministry, and/or congregation based on the material presented in this chapter?**

Your Accountability: **How and by whom do you want to be held accountable for taking these actions?**

Interlude

Don't Emulate. Excel.

Some years ago a service truck for Toshiba copiers passed me on the highway. I was struck by the motto displayed on the truck. "Don't copy. Lead." Being wholly committed to the vitality and vibrancy of congregations, I began to think about how that is true for congregations. Here is what dawned on me.

A *FaithSoaring* Church is about excelling rather than emulating. It is about leading rather than copying. Copying for congregations means to emulate other congregations. One congregation copies another because it sees in the original some signs of success or meaning it wants for itself. It is searching in other congregations for answers to its own vitality challenges. Without answers of its own, it looks elsewhere.

Leading for congregations means to excel in the unique and specific ways God is guiding your congregation. It answers these questions: "What is the unique purpose for which God brought our congregation into existence? Are we living into that purpose?" Leading is not a copying, cookie cutter, cloning approach.

Leading begins with an emerging understanding of God's spiritual strategic direction for your congregation. It is followed by taking risks to move forward in the direction you perceive God is leading you. Congregations constantly must discern how their actions honor the leadership of God.

Leading means to focus on the specific things you do extremely well as a congregation. Make these the model of quality and Christ-like love for your congregation. Leading focuses on the areas where your congregation has the greatest passion. Soar in these areas of your strength.

CHAPTER NINE

FaithSoaring Strategies

To journey in the direction of becoming a *FaithSoaring* Church, Christ the King, Trinity, and First used traditional long-range or strategic planning. Summit Heights and Nesmith used a Spiritual Strategic Journey approach. Experiential Missional Journey is the approach of choice for Lake Avenue and Midtown.

Reviewing the *FaithSoaring* nature of these congregations, let's remember that those who used long-range or strategic planning have not achieved the status of *FaithSoaring* Church. Both of the congregations who used a Spiritual Strategic Journey have become *FaithSoaring* Churches. Those using Experiential Missional Journey are a new wave of congregations well on their way to becoming *FaithSoaring* Churches.

Motivation to be *FaithSoaring* Churches

The first issue that must be addressed regarding *FaithSoaring* Church strategies is to determine if specific congregations who are not already *FaithSoaring* want to be *FaithSoaring*. Don't laugh. That is a serious question. In my 35 years of consulting with and coaching congregations I have found various perspectives on this issue.

It is the "why" question? Why do we need to change? What is wrong with the way things have been? Every time we try to change we cause more conflict. We like things the way they are. Congregations who cannot answer the "why" question will never be *FaithSoaring* unless they experience the direct, dramatic, divine intervention of God.

Here are some of the perspectives observed over the years.

Committed to *FaithSoaring*: Some congregations are already *FaithSoaring* and want to remain *FaithSoaring*. This is somewhat less than 20 percent of all congregations. In some denominational families this is typically only 10 to 15 percent. These congregations are often learners who are constantly looking for the next strategy, innovation, or tactic to help their congregation to continue to soar with faith. They want a sustained pattern of *FaithSoaring* and will work hard on Vision and Relationships to achieve this pattern. They are highly motivated.

Summit Heights and Nesmith fit this category because of their commitment to continually moving forward and looking for new opportunities to soar with faith. Summit Heights moves forward at a significant pace, and Nesmith at an incremental pace.

Once *FaithSoaring:* Some congregations were once *FaithSoaring,* but then their vision waned. They were so in love with the value and character of their ministry that they chose to continue the patterns which had been working for them. Some day they would like to be *FaithSoaring* again, but either they do not currently see the need or are unwilling to make the changes necessary to achieve a *FaithSoaring* status. The longer they wait, the more difficult it will be. It is doubtful they will be sufficiently motivated.

Trinity was once *FaithSoaring*. Then its geographic context began to experience radical transition and change. They focused on holding on to the way things had been, rather than seeing the transition and change as a new opportunity.

Pursuing *FaithSoaring:* These are congregations who have never been *FaithSoaring*. The reasons this has never happened are not important. Their desire to be *FaithSoaring* is the key issue. These congregations were named in chapter one as *Pursuing Congregations*. These are congregations who have the capacity, the readiness, and the opportunity to be *FaithSoaring*, and are intentionally moving in that direction. They are learners. They are motivated. They are looking to be captivated by an empowering Vision. They want a process that will result in deep ownership within their congregation for prophetic future ministry that soars with faith. They may very well have enough motivation to do this.

Lake Avenue is on a pursuing track. With the leadership of their pastoral team, the presence of the satellite campus of a university within site and an integral part of their ministry, and emerging resources with which to soar with faith, they are on a positive spiritual and strategic journey. It may be only a matter of time before they can be declared *FaithSoaring*.

Preparing for *FaithSoaring:* These congregations lack the capacity, readiness, and opportunity to be *FaithSoaring*. Yet, they say they want to be *FaithSoaring*. For them the issue will be readiness. Are they willing to do the things to build readiness within their congregation to soar with faith? Will they stick with the process long enough to become *FaithSoaring*? The full process for these congregations could easily be five to seven years. They are likely to experience some significant resistance from longer-term members of the congregation who cannot handle that much transition, change, and innovation. While they will have some motivation to be *FaithSoaring*, the journey will be tough.

In a way, this is Midtown. They are likely to be *FaithSoaring* by the time their reach Adulthood. Remember that congregations within their first generation of life should be thought of as potentially *FaithSoaring*. The reason is that we will not know until they face the identity and Vision crisis at the end of their first generation of life whether or not *FaithSoaring* patterns have been hardwired into their life and ministry, or if the high octane of their founding Vision is propelling them forward to a time they are only running on fumes. The assessment of the vitality of first generation congregations is another story for another time.

Lacking Motivation: A large number of congregations, perhaps a majority, lack the motivation to be *FaithSoaring*. At the same time they may on any given day claim they want to be *FaithSoaring*. When they come to understand the characteristics of *FaithSoaring* Churches, and the effort it will take to achieve this status, and the fact that they would have to choose a spiritual journey over a culturally-captive journey, they usually walk away as did the man in the Bible who had been rich from his youth up. This is sad, but true.

Christ the King and First are examples. Christ the King is well focused on being a congregation of high quality worship and spiritual formation, engages is loving social justice issues within its geographic context, and is led by Management. Its view of what a congregation ought to be doing is confined to these elements. First congregation lost the mantle of being the first or leading congregation of its denomination in its city more than two decades ago. It has never gotten over that, and hopes that tomorrow will bring a return of yesterday.

Making the Choice of Journey

The "how" question is answered through making a choice for the journey. How do you get from where we are to where God is leading us? How do we move beyond being at rest to being in movement? Even though we have been in movement for several years, we may not yet be *FaithSoaring*. How do we journey the additional required distance?

This book is not in its learning experience version seeking to address the details of the "how" question. It is providing a framework to begin the dialogue around why, how, and what. The challenge is that how a congregation becomes *FaithSoaring* must be discovered and developed one congregation at a time. There is no easy fix or obvious solution. It is a chaordic journey led by God and responded to by congregations.

If your congregation wants to move from where you are to *FaithSoaring*, what type of fuel do you need in your Lexus SUV? The answer is always high octane premium gasoline. This grade of fuel is available through engaging in either a Spiritual Strategic Journey or an Experiential Missionary Journey. These are brand names, of course, for spiritual and strategic processes offered by The Columbia Partnership that focus on right-brained, narrative approaches to envisioning a congregation's future. However, it is not the brand I want you to get from this chapter, but the concepts that underlie the processes. These are simply the brands I know best.

Other brands may also have the right fuel, as long as they address the synergy of the qualities of Vision, Relationships, Programs, and Management. I have often said that any credible, positive, and proactive process will work for congregations who are ready. No process will work for congregations who do not have a sense of urgency, and spiritual, strategic, leadership, and resources readiness. Among the issues any effective process should be able to address are as following:

1. Right-brained approaches that are more characteristic of people born after February 9, 1964 than those born before that date. People born before this date must be willing to transfer much authority and responsibility to these newer generations.

2. A process that is both spiritual and strategic in nature. It cannot be a business planning model.

3. A narrative approach that crafts a future story of ministry into which the congregation seeks to live.

4. A process that seeks to pull the congregation into the future rather than push the congregation into the future.

5. The congregation must already be proactively engaged in disciplemaking processes that help all youth and adults to mature in their faith, and to understand the unique call of God on their lives.

6. A focus on transitioning people in their relationships as the lead factor rather than a focus on changing things before transition actions and patterns have been hard wired into the congregation.

7. A clear plan to live into the future story of the congregation rather than to just produce a plan or deliverable that is then handed over to the same people who were not executing *FaithSoaring* strategies before.

8.   The creating of an Enduring Visionary Leadership Community composed of the senior or solo pastor, church ministerial and program staff, laypersons with deep passion for the future of the congregation under God's leadership, and laypersons with some passion plus the authority and influence to bring about change. [This community is referenced in chapter four.]

9.   Opportunities for ministry action followed by reflection on the implication of missional engagement for missional formation.

10.   Above all it must focus on the best possible synergy of Vision, Relationships, Programs, and Management.

The bottom line is that something like a Spiritual Strategic Journey or an Experiential Missional Journey may help your congregation to be *FaithSoaring*. Again, other processes that address the right quality issues and their synergy may be equally effective. It is important for congregations to use a process, and an outside consultant or coach, that fits their situation and with whom they can establish meaningful trust. These processes will favor Vision and Relationships over Programs and Management.

If *FaithSoaring* happens with long-range planning or strategic planning, then you know for sure God was in the process as He overcame the limitations of these approaches. Long-range planning and strategic planning tend to favor Programs and Management over Vision and Relationships. They may address Vision, but generally it is about a statement or motto rather than a movement.

Here is a quick overview of these various pathways.

Spiritual Strategic Journey

Spiritual Strategic Journey [SSJ] is a conceptual and feeling approach to being pulled forward into the future God has for congregations. The gospel it models is Luke. It focuses on a Visionary Leadership approach.

> **Purpose:** A Spiritual Strategic Journey process seeks to empower a congregational journey that is both spiritual and strategic in nature, and moves them in the direction of their full kingdom potential. They are pulled forward by God's future story of ministry for them as a congregation on mission. The goal is to live into their future story of ministry as a congregational movement.
> The sourcebook for the journey is my book **Pursuing the Full Kingdom Potential of Your Congregation**, and should be read by every member of the Enduring Visionary Leadership Community who is driving and navigating the journey.

> **Readiness:** Before the SSJ process can begin it is necessary for a congregation to determine their readiness for the process and the journey, and their willingness and commitment to engage in the full process.

> **Seasons:** A Spiritual Strategic Journey process has three seasons: *Spiritual Season, Strategic Season*, and *Journey Season*. Each season lasts around 120 days, although the journey is really only beginning and is the ongoing aspect of the SSJ process.

> • *Spiritual Season*: This season is about transition in the relationship of the congregation with God, one another in the congregation, and the context in which the congregation serves. The primary activity is 100 Days of Discernment.

- ***Strategic Season:*** This season is about determining the changes that need to be made. The primary activity is crafting the Future Story of the congregation.

- ***Journey Season:*** This season is about taking the journey in the direction of God's full kingdom potential for your congregation. The primary activity is developing the Future Story Fulfillment Map and to begin living into the Future Story.

Outcome: The outcome of the SSJ process is a dynamic, ever-changing Future Story of what will characterize the congregation ten years into the future, a Future Story Fulfillment Map that is an operational plan for the first one to three years, and a congregation committed to live into their Future Story.

Impact: The impact of the SSJ process is not only clarity of direction and a purposeful future, but congregational leadership committed to living into that direction.

Experiential Missional Journey

Experiential Missional Journey [EMJ] is a perceptual and feeling approach to being pulled forward into the future God has for congregations. The gospel it models is Mark. It is an action then reflection approach. It focuses on a Relationship Experiences approach.

Purpose: An Experiential Missional Journey process seeks to empower a congregational journey that is based on a missional action then reflection approach, and moves churches in the direction of being a fully missional congregation. They are pulled forward by God's future story of ministry for them as a missional congregation. The goal is to live into their future story as a missional congregation.

Readiness: Before the EMJ process can begin it is necessary for a congregation to determine their readiness for the process and the journey, and their willingness and commitment to engage in the full process.

Seasons: An Experiential Missional Journey process has three seasons: *Experiential Season, Formation Season*, and *Journey Season*. Each season lasts around 120 days, although the journey is really only beginning and is the ongoing aspect of the EMJ process.

- ***Experiential Season:*** This season is about engaging at least 50 percent of the active congregation in projects that are missional in nature, or that support these projects. A support activity is 100 Days of Discernment. It supports the 100 Days of Missional Engagement. Unlike the SSJ process, the EMJ process takes 240 days in Pre-Season to be prepared to launch the Experiential Season.

- ***Formation Season:*** This season is about reflecting on the *Experiential Season*, and crafting the Future Story of the congregation as a missional congregation.

- ***Journey Season:*** This season is about taking the journey in the direction of God's full kingdom potential for your congregation. The primary activity is developing the Future Story Fulfillment Map and to begin living into the Future Story.

Outcome: The outcome of the EMJ process is a dynamic, ever-changing Future Story of what will characterize the congregational transition and change, a Future Story Fulfillment Map that is an operational plan for the first one to three years, and a congregation committed to live into their Future Story.

Impact: The impact of the SSJ process is not only clarity of direction and a purposeful future, but congregational leadership committed to living into that direction.

Long-Range or Strategic Planning

Long-Range and Strategic Planning represent what are now traditional approaches to pushing a congregation forward into the future. Long-Range planning is a perceptual and logical approach characteristic of the gospel of Matthew. Strategic Planning is a conceptual and logical approach characteristic of the gospel of John.

They place emphasis on Programs and Management. As such, they move Management into the driver's seat and Programs into the navigator's seat. This leaves Vision and Relationships in the back seat. Such a configuration will never empower a congregation to become *FaithSoaring*. Yet it is the default position for many congregations.

This approach ends up focusing more on the short-term than the long-term, tactics more than a few impactful priorities, outputs rather than impacts, tradition rather than innovation, measurement with metrics rather than stories, and checklists that are completed rather than new discoveries that enhance the journey.

At the same time, long-range or strategic planning may be the first or second right step for a congregation on the aging side of the congregational life cycle who has been at rest or wandering in the wilderness for a minimum of five to seven years. To leap forward into a process that focuses on Vision and Relationships may be too big of a step in the short-term. Perhaps it needs practice at allowing God to help it project a positive, creative future that soars with faith. Perhaps it needs to be moving for a while before it can clearly hear, see, taste, smell, and touch the perfect leadership of God.

However, remember this is about the congregation's lack of faith and not God's lack of leadership of the congregation. I am convinced that God wants every congregation to reach its full kingdom potential and to be continually *FaithSoaring*. How about you? What do you think?

Coaching Insights for Chapter Nine

Personal Reflections for Learners

What methodologies has your congregation used to project the future and move forward? Have they helped you achieve a *FaithSoaring* status?

What pathways and actions are you willing to engage in to achieve a *FaithSoaring* status?

If you are currently a *FaithSoaring* Church, what steps are you taking to sustain this status and continuing as Perfecting congregation?

Your Reflections: What are your reflections on the material presented in this chapter?

Your Actions: What actions do you need to take about your life, ministry, and/or congregation based on the material presented in this chapter?

Your Accountability: How and by whom do you want to be held accountable for taking these actions?

Interlude

Pulling, Not Pushing

A very difficult concept to grasp about a *FaithSoaring* Church is that it involves pulling rather than pushing. Pushing is hard. Particularly when pushing an object up a hill. Pulling is easy if you know how to leverage your strengths with the right combination of pulleys.

Even the image of hot air balloons soaring increasingly higher does not fully illustrate this concept. We are generally looking up from underneath the balloons, which may imply pushing. In the true spirit of pulling we should be looking back from beyond the balloons as we watch them approach us.

A colleague of mine in The Columbia Partnership, Dick Hamm, recently reminded me of an image that speaks well to pulling versus pushing. It involves the aerodynamics of the wing of on airplane. The top of an airplane wing is curved. As air rushes over the top of the wing it is lighter and moving faster than the air under the wing. This action creates lift and allows the airplane to be literally pulled into the sky.

When we concentrate on the engines pushing the airplane down the runway, we forget they may provide the forward motion, but they do not provide the lifting action. In the same way the lift of a wing pulls an airplane into the sky, the lift of God's spiritual strategic direction for your congregation can lift it to heights you may never have considered. You become a pulling congregation rather than a pushing congregation.

If you find yourself exhausted from pushing, relax and allow God to pull your congregation forward into a God-led future. You will find this a lot easier to do than you have thought. *FaithSoaring* Churches are pulled.

Part Three

Leadership for *FaithSoaring* Churches

Part Three takes the *FaithSoaring* Churches concept and applies it in related arenas. First is around individual leaders. Second is around leadership communities. Third is around the denominational entities that relate to congregations.

Here is a brief executive summary for each chapter.

Chapter Ten: *FaithSoaring* Leaders

This chapter describes the characteristics of *FaithSoaring* Leaders, and some of the things that do not characterize them. It then more specifically addresses senior or solo pastors, congregational staff, and lay volunteers. These three categories at their best function as an Enduring Visionary Leadership Community.

Chapter Eleven: *FaithSoaring* Leadership Communities

This chapter advocates that a best practice approach to *FaithSoaring* leadership is *FaithSoaring* Leadership Communities. This requires abandoning committees, skipping teams, and embracing leadership communities. As leadership communities soar with excellence, they help empower *FaithSoaring* Churches.

Chapter Twelve: *FaithSoaring* Denominations

This chapter focuses on *FaithSoaring* Denominations and the dilemmas they face, the various types of denominations that exist, and solutions that will indeed empower them to be *FaithSoaring*. This chapter intentionally provides only an overview to a very complex issue, and introduces a few of the aspects of this issue. Perhaps a book on *FaithSoaring* Denominations is in our future.

CHAPTER TEN

FaithSoaring Leaders

Way too few leaders are *FaithSoaring*. They lead by sight rather than by faith. They lead with the short-term in mind rather than the long-term. They are captivated by the tyranny of the urgent rather than the democracy of the patient. Their Vision is myopic rather than farsighted. In their weakness they are afraid to ask for help whereas strong leaders enjoy help when they cannot figure out what is next.

Leaders in this chapter refer to the senior or solo pastor, staff, and lay volunteers. These ideally compose the Enduring Visionary Leadership Community. In situations where they do not get *FaithSoaring* Leadership they form the Enduring Reactionary Management Committee. I guess technically they could also form the Enduring Leadership Management Community or the Enduring Reactionary Leadership Committee. But I digress.

Oh, let me digress a little more. An Enduring Reactionary Management Committee believes that tight, boxed, efficient, and strictly Accountable Management will move the congregation forward into the future. [They may also believe the world is flat.] This belief confuses a congregation with an organization. A congregation is a spiritual organism led by God, so business organizational principles do not translate easily into Christ-centered, faith-based organisms. They do translate. They just require a wise interpreter.

FaithSoaring Leaders Are Like This

The hope is that congregational leaders will indeed function as *FaithSoaring* Leaders. If they do, the following will be some of their characteristics.

1. They give clear evidence that they are walking by faith rather than by sight. They see potential with their heart, soul, mind, and strength when it is not otherwise obvious. They step out into darkness with faith knowing God has already gone before them. Therefore, it is not a risk, but an assurance. They remember it was not raining when Noah built the ark.

2. Their actions show a clear focus on Vision and Relationships. They know that Visionary Leadership must be the mantra of vital and vibrant congregations and ministries. Relationship Experiences is where they focus their time and most crucial resources. They know that what ultimately matters is the relationship of people with God, one another, and the context in which they serve and the worldwide context of God's world.

3.   They are obviously captivated by God's empowering Vision for their ministry and that of their congregation. It is obvious they are somewhat a radical in that they are tenaciously committed to fulfilling the Vision God has given them and their congregation or ministry. They are always asking people they lead how every action will help the congregation or ministry live into their Vision.

4.   They focus on the strengths of the congregation or ministry they serve. They have a bias towards affirming what is right, good, and loving and build on it. They are investigative leaders. They are constantly looking around their congregation or ministry to discover and develop strengths.

5.   Their own personal style of leadership is strengths-based. Over a long season they find ways to minister with their **StandOut** strengths, and empower others to lead with their strengths. They do not shirk the responsibility of leadership to address a multiplicity of issues. Instead they recognize the diversity of gifts needed in their congregation and ministry, and raise up people with those gifts and strengths to make sure there is passionate leadership in all places needing leadership.

6.   They strive for excellence, and to reach their full kingdom potential as a leader. They do this in the contextual setting from which they have been called to serve. They learn principles from other congregations and ministries. They possess passion which impacts the unique circumstances of their ministry setting. They continually innovate, always seeking to perfect what they are doing. They pace the speed and distance of their daily, weekly, monthly, and annual journey as suggested by the 20 Mile March in the book **Great by Choice**.

7.   Whatever they do they do with the highest possible quality. They seek to do everything well, rather than trying to do everything they can imagine but only do it with mediocrity. They do not call people to be faithful participants in Programmatic Emphases, but to be effective disciples with a missional focus.

8.   They are committed to a missional life style that seeks to cross barriers to love all who need to experience the unconditional love of Jesus. They seek to continually discover the people to whom they have been sent, what their needs are, and how they can develop the capacities to minister to them. They forget about what they can do to people in ministry that makes them feel proud. Rather, they learn what they can do to lift up the people to whom they have been sent.

9.   They have high, yet reasonable, expectations of their life and ministry, and high, yet reasonable, expectations of the people they lead. They expect to continue growing in the grace and knowledge of our Lord and Savior Jesus Christ. That is an intentional journey for them. They expect the same of those they lead.

10.   They lead with a prayerful attitude that is always seeking to glorify and praise God in all they do, without being prideful. Their worship of God is not a scheduled event they attend once or twice each week. It is a daily attitude and practice as they pray without ceasing.

Are these the right ten characteristics? Perhaps. Are there more? Yes. There are even whole other ways of looking at the *FaithSoaring* characteristics of leaders in the church and ministry world. One way is to focus primarily on biblical and spiritual characteristics. Another is on values and character.

FaithSoaring Leaders Are Not Like This

One way to narrow the focus as to who are *FaithSoaring* Leaders is to indicate characteristics not held by them.

1. *FaithSoaring* Leaders do not have a Messianic Complex. They do not believe they are the savior of their congregation, and if they do not save it then it will not be saved. They have a balanced and healthy perspective about their own ability to lead and affect transition and change in the congregation that may lead to transformation.

2. *FaithSoaring* Leaders do not have a Rescuer Mentality. They care deeply for people, debilitating life situations, and personal crises. But, they are not constantly getting mired down with dysfunctional people and situations which drain their energies, and thus make them unable to help healthy people take the next steps in their spiritual pilgrimage.

3. *FaithSoaring* Leaders are not risky in the sense that they are always taking risks without counting the costs. They have the wisdom to know when to take risks and not to take risks. They know how to appropriately gauge the intensity of their actions to fit the situation.

4. *FaithSoaring* Leaders are not controlled by Management and the people who prefer Management over the other three qualities. They can give away Management tasks, and yet in the way they assign or delegate them they appropriately position them as support tasks rather than core Vision tasks. They are not personally threatened by or accommodate to overbearing Management people.

Senior or Solo Pastors

It is not a safe assumption that all pastors are naturally *FaithSoaring*. They are not. I cannot give you a figure as to how many are *FaithSoaring*, but I suspect it is not all that different than the number of congregations I estimate are *FaithSoaring*. That number is 20 percent. How many pastors do you think are *FaithSoaring*?

It is important for pastors to have self-awareness on whether they lead best with heart, soul, mind, strength. This will reveal if they best express Visionary Leadership, Relationship Experiences, Programmatic Emphases, or Accountable Management. Any of these four can be the foundation for pastors to be *FaithSoaring* Leaders if they understand the need for a synergy of the four qualities, and are able to raise up leaders with other perspectives to create a balanced approach.

As the Chief Visionary Officer, the senior or solo pastor must be the voice of Vision regardless of whether or not they are gifted in Visionary Leadership. It comes with the role. They must use their preaching teaching, and other opportunities to coach individuals and leadership communities to cast and clarify vision. They must be one of the key persons continually asking the question about every new proposed strategy or tactic—"How will this help us fulfill our vision?"

Senior or solo pastors in *FaithSoaring* Churches are able to focus their time around the issues of Vision, Relationships, Programs, and Management. The ideal is that they can spend 60 to 80 percent of their time and effort focused on Vision and Relationships. The needed commitment to Programs and Management would be handled by congregational staff and lay volunteers.

Congregational Staff

It is not a safe assumption that all congregational staff are naturally *FaithSoaring*. They are not. How many do you think are *FaithSoaring*? Just as with pastors, it is important for congregational staff to have self-awareness on whether they lead best with heart, soul, mind, or strength. Visionary Leadership, Relationship Experiences, Programmatic Emphases, or Accountable Management can all be the foundation for congregational staff to be

FaithSoaring Leaders if they understand the need for a synergy of the four qualities, and are able to raise up volunteer leaders with other perspectives to create a balanced approach.

Congregational staff in *FaithSoaring* Churches shoulder much of the responsibility for Programs, but also have significant responsibilities in Relationships. They should be able to focus 60 to 80 percent of their time in these two areas. They also have support roles to Vision and Management.

Conflict between congregational staff and their senior pastor often occurs when there is a *FaithSoaring* leadership imbalance. This imbalance is not easy to define or describe as there are so many intangibles related to it. Here are several typical situations:

1.   The senior pastor is a *FaithSoaring* Leader, for the most part. One limitation the pastor may have is the lack of capacity to help her/his staff to also be *FaithSoaring* Leaders. The pastor may even have impatience surrounding this issue. This will particularly be the case with staff who were in the congregation before the current pastor began.

2.   The senior pastor is not a *FaithSoaring* Leader, but one or more staff persons are *FaithSoaring* Leaders. In many cases this is a train wreck waiting to happen. Cutting to the chase, the reality is that the staff persons must adjust in this case or find themselves undercutting the leadership of the senior pastor and playing into the hands of selected laypersons who may not be affirming of the senior pastor's leadership. In some cases the staff persons need to find another place of leadership.

3.   The senior pastor nor the staff persons are *FaithSoaring* Leaders. Yet they see themselves as *FaithSoaring* Leaders. Their self-perception does not conform to reality. Therefore, they are like a leader who has lost her/his personal ministry vision. They work hard and accomplish less. Their stress level rises and they become conflict creators and contributors. It is either hard for them to work together as a team, or they work amazingly well as a team because they do not understand the reality of their situation.

Lay Volunteers

It is equally important that at least 20 percent of lay volunteers are *FaithSoaring* Leaders. When laypersons are *FaithSoaring* Leaders, they are passionate about their congregation moving forward by means of a God-led journey. They want the Vision of the congregation to be fulfilled. They want to reach their full kingdom potential as a congregation.

They do not want controlling Management to get in the way of progress. They have a time dimension within the congregation that does look at the heritage, acknowledge the present movement of God, and reach for a future that only comes from the heart of God.

Lay volunteers who are in the zone concerning the forward progress of the congregation resonate with understanding a multiplicity of leadership styles that involve leading with heart, soul, mind, and strength. They want to use their spiritual gifts, strengths and skills, and personality preferences to help their congregation be a *FaithSoaring* Church.

Lay volunteers typically will spend 60 to 80 percent of their time in Programs and Management. For their congregation to be a *FaithSoaring* Church, they must simultaneously realize that they must understand and support Vision and Relationships as they conduct their work.

They are willing to engage in loving coaching and even confrontation of fellow and sister laypersons who want the congregation to go back to the way things were, or to keep as sacrifice spiritual practices that have substantially lost their spiritual nature and have become cultural practices. They are willing to give permission for the continual innovation of the congregation.

Conflict for *FaithSoaring* Leaders who are lay volunteers often comes when there is a mismatch of their depth of passion with a perceived lack of passion on the part of the senior or solo pastor, and any congregational staff. Such situations will test their emotional and spiritual maturity.

Coaching Insights for Chapter Ten

Personal Reflections for Learners

Which of the characteristics of *FaithSoaring* Leaders would you claim as a characteristic of your leadership?

How are you expressing these characteristics in your congregational leadership role?

What is your reaction to the things that do not characterize *FaithSoaring* Leaders? Which, if any, of those characteristics do you possess?

In what ways is your leadership role contributing to the synergy of Vision, Relationships, Programs, and Management?

Your Reflections: What are your reflections on the material presented in this chapter?

Your Actions: What actions do you need to take about your life, ministry, and/or congregation based on the material presented in this chapter?

Your Accountability: How and by whom do you want to be held accountable for taking these actions?

Interlude

Can Smaller Membership Churches Soar?

FaithSoaring Church. Is that just for mega churches? When churches soar with their strengths, do they become larger? If so, is *FaithSoaring* just another word for church growth? Can small churches soar? The answers are no, maybe, no, and yes.

No. *FaithSoaring* Church is not just for mega churches. Size is not the issue. Purpose is the issue. Solid doctrinal beliefs are the issue. Meaningful worship is the issue. Engaging fellowship is the issue. Ever deepening discipleship is the issue. Missions and evangelism are the issues.

Maybe. Churches who are purposeful, who focus their ministry around their collective spiritual gifts and their leadership strengths, are probably more effective in their life and ministry. This effectiveness may also result in numerical growth. But it is not always that simple and straightforward.

No. Church growth and *FaithSoaring* Church are not the same thing. *FaithSoaring* Church is about being led forward by faith rather than by sight. It means your church sees with its spiritual heart and not its physical eyes, into a future only God knows for sure.

Yes. Smaller membership churches can soar. They are the best examples of *FaithSoaring* Church when they have an increasingly clearer sense of God's spiritual strategic direction for them. Such a direction leads them to engage in evangelism, missions, ministry, discipleship, worship, and fellowship that honor God the Father, Son, and Holy Spirit.

CHAPTER ELEVEN

FaithSoaring Leadership Communities

Because *FaithSoaring* Leadership Communities tend to be more characteristic in organizations with leaders born after February 9, 1964, when the Baby Busters started appearing, such communities are more present in Summit Heights and Midtown than in any of the other five congregations. Lake Avenue and Christ the King are both working in this direction. But Nesmith, Trinity, and First do not see the need for moving from their board and committee structure.

FaithSoaring Churches are best served by *FaithSoaring* Leadership Communities composed of clergy, or laity, or both. Leadership communities are not boards, committees, or teams. They are an emerging form of clustering leaders that ought to be a part of *FaithSoaring* Churches.

FaithSoaring Leadership Communities wrestle constantly with the dichotomy of harmony and diversity. If these communities are composed of people who were born within ten years of one another, have been attending this congregation approximately the same amount of time, have substantially the same approach to major Christian doctrines, and attend the same worship service if the congregation has multiple worship services, then harmony will be easy to achieve. It will be even easier if they are in compatible friendship networks within the congregation. Harmony is easier to achieve among people who have the same or similar perspectives. Yet it may also be shallow and myopic.

If, however, the people who are part of a leadership community are of different birth generations, have been attending the congregation for a significantly different number of years, have some very distinctive Christian doctrinal perspectives, and attend a different worship service, then their diversity will make harmony more difficult to achieve. Yet once achieved it is stronger, deeper, and perhaps longer lasting.

FaithSoaring Leadership Communities are not so much concerned about reaching common ground on issues, but discovering higher ground that is the result of collaborative discernment of God's leadership. Common ground involves compromise, bargaining, negotiation, and loss that both parties will try at some future date to gain back. Higher ground involves collaboration, synergy, innovation, and new ways of working.

Abandon Committees, Skip Teams, and Embrace Communities

Does it seem that many congregations are late adapters to some trends? It does to me. It appears congregations are just getting around to adapting to certain trends as the next trend is emerging. For example, organizing congregations according to teams rather than committees continues in its ascendancy, just as in the world at-large teams are fading in favor of communities.

It is a positive step that congregations are abandoning committees for teams. But what if congregations were to skip the team phase and embrace communities? Too radical? Perhaps so! Too cutting edge? Hardly!

Leadership communities and learning communities are the next wave of congregational leadership, governance, and missional engagement. Are you ready to empower the transition and change? Consider seven differences between committees, teams, and communities as you think about making the transition.

As you consider these seven, let's acknowledge an important point. This material is talking generically about the three group forms—committees, teams, and communities. It is also suggesting that communities are the way congregations and other organizations should ideally operate when they are *FaithSoaring*. At the same time many congregations and other organizations use the titles of committees, teams, and communities without having the same definitions and distinctions presented below. Some committees may operate very well as teams. Some teams are great communities. Some communities fall into mediocre patterns and seem like committees. Just saying!

Difference One—Formation: *Committees* tend to be elected or appointed in keeping with the bylaws, policies, or polity of congregations. *Teams* are recruited or drafted to work on a specific task or set of tasks. *Communities* are voluntarily connected in search of genuine and meaningful experiences. For communities it is always relationship before task. Communities often form before they have a task. Later they adopt a task or cause, permanently or for a season.

Difference Two—Focus: *Committees* focus on making decisions or setting policies. *Teams* focus on maturing to the point that they become high task performance groups. *Communities* add qualitative relationships, meaning, and experiences to the organizations, organisms, or movements to which they are connected. Storytelling is a great action that characterizes the work and ministry of communities.

Difference Three—Membership: *Committees* tend to have a fixed term of membership. *Teams* may have a defined term of membership, or may serve until a certain set of tasks is completed. *Communities* have no bounded membership and people tend to come and go based on their continuing interest in the journey. Ad hoc is a legitimate way to refer to communities. They are constantly changing size, composition, and place.

Difference Four—Outside Assistance: *Committees* seek high quality training events or consultants if they need outside assistance. *Teams* partner with respected practitioners or coaches. *Communities* align with champions or advocates who come alongside them in long-term relationships. Ministry coaching is a leadership skill from which communities often benefit; particularly process coaching rather than content coaching is more characteristic of teams. Process coaching helps communities effectively move forward with the actions around which they have passion. Content coaching provides communities with the substance (content) for the projects around which they have passion.

Difference Five—Recruitment: *Committees* look for people of position who can bring to the committee or council the influence needed to get the work of the committee respected by people of power in the congregation. *Teams* look for people of expertise who have the gifts, skills and preferences to complete a task or set of tasks. *Communities* look for people of passion who want to have fun helping to bring exciting experiences to congregational participants, and a spiritual strategic journey or experiential missional journey to the congregation.

Difference Six—Benefits: *Committees* benefit congregations by building ownership and loyalty for the mission of the congregation. *Teams* benefit congregations by providing more effective action more quickly than committees. *Communities* benefit congregations by providing more enthusiasm and meaningful relationships within congregations. Often in the short-term they provide more effective action. The long-term requires great coaching of communities.

Difference Seven—Style of Work: *Committees* focus on making decisions that are lasting and manage the resources of the congregation efficiently at the best price. *Teams* focus on debating the strengths and weaknesses of the various choices to complete a task, and typically end up with the highest quality product or outcome. *Communities* dialogue, engage in discernment activities, and arrive at the best solutions for a particular opportunity or challenge. Actions to move forward generally occur simultaneous to the dialogue and discernment process rather than following sequentially.

Is your congregation ready to embrace communities? The following is a presentation on this concept that focuses on middle judicatories or regional denominational organizations. This is an arena where I have been applying this concept most frequently. Implications for congregations follow in the next section.

A Networked Ministry Organization From a Regional Denominational Perspective

When a congregation or other Christian ministry organization is organized around communities rather than teams or committees, it may become a networked ministry organization. This is a key characteristic for some *FaithSoaring* Churches. It definitely works at Summit Heights and Midtown, but other factors probably enter into its success in these two congregations.

Is it possible? Is it needed? Would it better empower our work? Is it a step forward? Do we understand it? Do we see it as progress? Will it help us make more sense of denominational structures in the 21st century? Will it allow younger generations to see more relevance in congregational or denominational structures? How will it help us fulfill our future vision of ministry? Does it have the possibility of raising up more leadership within our congregational or denominational organization or judicatory? Who will be the winners? Who will be the losers? It is possible we would all win? Will it flatten our structure? Where is accountability?

All of these are legitimate questions to ask as any congregation, judicatory, or dimension of denominational life considers a networked denominational structure. They should be asked by clergy and lay congregational leaders, denominational staff, the board of regional denominational organizations, and even national/international denominational structures who would also be impacted by this shift.

Let's consider a foundation for this concept, leadership communities, and learning communities as it might work in a regional denominational organization seeking to be a networked organization. As you read this, consider the applications of this for *FaithSoaring* Churches.

A Foundation for a Networked Organization

During recent decades several national/international denominations in North America have moved from a centralized or hierarchical form of organizational structure to a decentralized or shared form of organization. A few denominations are considering or experimenting with distributive systems or becoming a networked denomination.

Centralized: This form of governance and authority can be represented by a hub and a spoke concept. Governance is controlled by the hub. Authority rests primarily in the hub. Spokes go out from the hub to various constituent groups. The primary constituent groups are churches, but may also include other organizational expressions of the denominational structure. A formal rim is seldom attached by the hub to complete the construction of a wheel. The hub desires to keep authority, responsibility, and relationships directly to the hub.

The primary focus of a centralized structure is on the hub. Congregations and other organizational expressions exist to serve the hub or the core denomination at the regional or judicatory dimension. The hub may also be part of a series of hubs and spokes related to the national/international denominational structure. As such, it seeks to be a gatekeeper of the relationship of churches and other regional/judicatory organizational expressions regarding the national/international denominational organization.

Decentralized: This form of governance and authority begins with a complete wheel composed of a hub, spokes, and a rim. Relationships along the rim are encouraged; even initiated. Clusters of relationships along the rim emerge spontaneously or by intentional action by the hub and/or the spokes. Some responsibility and resources are given by the hub to the clusters of relationships to empower greater grassroots or affinity action and effectiveness. However, authority still rests with the hub, and the hub can seek to withdraw responsibility and resources at any time.

The primary focus of a decentralized structure is still on the hub, but some shared leadership situations are allowed or intentionally created. Congregations are more the focus of the work and ministry of regional or judicatory dimension than in a centralized system. The hub remains a point on a spoke related to the national/international denominational structure. As such, it seeks to be a gatekeeper of the relationship of churches and other regional/judicatory organizational expressions regarding the national/international denominational organization

Networked: This form of governance and authority can best be represented by the diagram below. It is called a distributive system in physics. It is commonly called a network. Its two primary parts are nodes and connectors. There is no central hub. Nodes represent various things—the judicatory/regional denominational governance and staff, various organizational expressions, collaborating networks, and most especially the churches. The connectors carry core values, authority, responsibilities, and relationships throughout the network.

Rather than being presented as the hub of the system, the judicatory/regional denominational structure is represented by one or more specialized nodes known as correlating nodes. Congregations and other organizational expressions voluntarily create clusters or the next dimensions of networks around various relationships, causes, or other affinity identifiers. The spiritual and strategic elements of the future story of the judicatory or regional denominational structure can be represented by one or more nodes.

The primary focus of a networked structure is on the nodes; particularly the churches. The judicatory or regional denominational node or nodes seek to correlate the work of the churches within the core value, authority, responsibilities, and relationships present and needed. Rather than being overly organizational in nature, a networked regional denomination is an organism or a living movement.

Networks are intended to be characterized by adult-to-adult relationships, whereas in centralized or decentralized structures there are definite parent-child and parent-adolescent relationships respectively. Thus, the term correlating node is used to refer to the work in a network of what in centralized or decentralized structures is called the hub. Coordination often implies over-under. Correlation is intended to imply beside or alongside in the sense of the Holy Spirit coming alongside us.

The basic organization of a network is illustrated here:

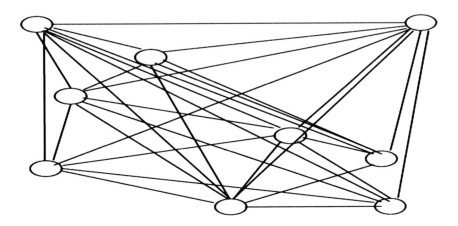

The nodes are socio-religious communities of two types: 1. Leadership Communities, and 2. Learning Communities. These are general categories and generic titles. Specific communities usually take on names that more clearly define their focus or what they do.

Leadership Communities

The nature or manner of leadership communities is to engage in correlation or collaboration. Key actions are spiritual formation, vision casting, and storytelling. Storytelling is the key currency of networked organizations.

Core functions are generally two: visionary leadership and empowering management. Visionary leadership addresses mission, purpose, values, and vision. Empowering management addresses essential administration and support for visionary leadership.

Learning Communities

The nature or manner of learning communities is to be entrepreneurial and proactive. Key actions are networking, vision fulfillment, and storytelling. Relationships are the key currency of learning communities, and always come before tasks.

Core functions are generally two: relationships, and programs, projects, or processes. Relationships address the formation of community, and out of that collaborative engagement. Programs, projects, and processes address missional engagement, capacity building, and multiplication of the next dimension of networks.

Implications for *FaithSoaring* Churches

The implications are several for *FaithSoaring* Churches seeking to function as a networked organization:

1. A centralized form of governance and authority is good for maintaining a focus on Programs and Management. It provides stability for institutionally organized congregations. Like a heart pacemaker, it guarantees a minimum level of functioning for a congregation. It provides for adherence to principles and practices that sustain historically proven doctrine, polity, and practice. It is not likely to result in a focus on Vision and Relationships. It keeps the functioning of congregation within a figurative box. Faithfulness is a key word for these congregations.

2. A decentralized form of governance and authority allows a congregation to experiment with things outside the box or even beyond the box, while maintaining a center, core or boxed identity. Historically proven doctrine, polity, and practice is still at the core of the life and ministry of the congregation. Yet added to faithfulness is the word effectiveness as the congregation is willing to give permission for leaders and leadership communities to experiment with more effective forms of programs, ministries, and activities. A focus on Vision and Relationships that may inform the governance and authority is empowered.

3. A networked or distributive form of governance provides the opportunity to soar with faith. It focuses on faithfulness, effectiveness, and innovation. It moves sufficiently outside and beyond the box that a center is no longer present, and the box is not relevant. It fully empowers an interdependent network that encourages creativity, depth, experimentation, and doing new things in new ways with new forms focused on new people. Yet, at the same time the word interdependent is essential as congregations continue to be primary community for many people connected with them.

4. Networked or distributed congregations are led by leadership communities rather than boards or committees by whatever name fits each denominational family. These leadership communities handle the Management issues in full support of Vision. Often they are able to embody or be captivated by Vision and provide critical visionary leadership while they address essential administration. They continually tell the stories of the full congregation organism to the congregational participants and the world outside the congregation.

5. Networked or distributed congregations use learning communities to organize movements around Relationships and Programs. These learning communities are fully empowered to act within the core values of the congregation in the direction of the fulfillment of the Vision of the congregation. One of their key independent responsibilities is to tell the stories within and without the congregation of what God is doing in and through their programs, ministries, and activities. Accountability is to one another, and the core values and Vision of the congregation.

Coaching Insights for Chapter Eleven

Personal Reflections for Learners

How are leadership groups best expressed in your congregation—committees, teams, or communities? Why have you chosen this particular expression? Are you happy with it? Do you need to transition to another form?

How is group leadership—whether committees, teams, or communities—helping to empower *FaithSoaring* in your congregation?

How is your model of group leadership allowing for the positive expression of spiritual gifts, strengths/skills, and preferences?

Your Reflections: **What are your reflections on the material presented in this chapter?**

Your Actions: **What actions do you need to take about your life, ministry, and/or congregation based on the material presented in this chapter?**

Your Accountability: **How and by whom do you want to be held accountable for taking these actions?**

Interlude

Do You Know the Next Steps?

I know a secret. Actually, my secret is widely known. But it's a secret because ministers are not supposed to talk about it. Here it is.

Many pastors are clueless as to what next steps to take in leadership. This is true even in what appear to be the most successful pastors in the most successful congregations. They have done everything they know how to do. They have used every ministry tool they learned in seminary, at conferences, in books, from speakers, and from personal mentors in ministry.

How do they express their sense of being clueless? Through anger and despair. In anger they try to make their denomination be different and follow their image of church. In despair they burn out, self-destruct, or become ineffective; some even leave Christian ministry.

For these people *FaithSoaring* Church seems like a fantasy rather than a challenge. At the very time they need to increase their dependence on the Triune God, they have difficulty feeling God's presence in their life and ministry.

The larger part of the secret is that many laypersons—probably a higher percentage than pastors—are clueless as to the next forward steps for their congregation. Too often laypersons see the next steps as the return to yesterday when things were better in the church. Or perhaps they think implementing specific management tactics will make things right in their congregation.

Neither of these are the character of a *FaithSoaring* Church. It is extremely difficult, if not impossible, to have a *FaithSoaring* Church if the leaders are not *FaithSoaring*.

CHAPTER TWELVE

FaithSoaring Denominations

FaithSoaring Churches have various types of relationships with denominations. First Church is a pillar of support for their denomination with multiple people from the congregation serving on various boards and committees in the national, regional, and local dimensions of the denomination. Nesmith and Trinity are very active in their local and regional denominational organizations. The pastor and several laypersons from Christ the King are officers in their middle judicatory. Lake Avenue has a deep partnership with their denomination because they are a redevelopment congregation.

The launch of Midtown was significantly funded by their denomination, and it is also acting as a church planting incubation center for multiple congregations within and beyond their denomination. Summit Heights recently withdrew from their denomination and is part of a national contemporary congregation affinity group. They are not hostile to their denomination, but simply could not see what benefits they were receiving from the relationship.

Way too few denominations are *FaithSoaring* Denominations. Way too many are focused on Programmatic Events and Accountable Management. Too few are focused on Visionary Leadership and Relationship Experiences. Too many are plateaued and declining. Too many are becoming less real to the movement of congregations within their tribe.

More regional denominational organizations, also known in many denominations as middle judicatories, are *FaithSoaring* in nature than are their national or international denominational equivalents. New, emerging denominations are more likely to be *FaithSoaring.* Unfortunately some of these are splits out of larger denominations some of whom have been in existence for more than 100 years.

Denominations who are *FaithSoaring* have strong Visionary Leadership and Relationship Experiences, and understand the need to renew their core while extending their ministry. This means they know they need to annually have an increasing number of congregations, leaders, and leadership and learning communities to be *FaithSoaring.* A good number of denominations have excellent values and emphases, but they forget they need to renew the core, and engender *FaithSoaring*, or they will outrun their ministry supply lines. It is a dilemma.

The Dilemma: Unreal Denominations

Too often denominations respond to the challenges they face by choosing the route of fixing something through technical leadership, rather than transforming something through adaptive leadership. [For more information on how this concept applies to church organizations see ***Recreating the Church: Leadership for the Postmodern Age*** by Richard Hamm. St. Louis: Chalice Press, 2007.] They are unreal in relationship to their congregations rather than real and genuine. They typically have one or more of the following characteristics, or take some of the following actions.

1. They still believe congregations exist to serve denominations, rather than denominations existing to serve congregations. They have forgotten the basic image that congregational movements are like a cloud, and denominational organizations are like a box. The cloud created the box. The box did not create the cloud. The cloud is constantly moving, changing size, and changing shape. The box is at rest unless intentionally picked up and moved. Denominations fall behind congregations unless they intentionally move and are agile.

2. Denominations seek to transform by constantly restructuring. The primary mid- to long-term impact of restructuring by denominational organizations is to position themselves for the next restructuring. For some reason denominational organizations have never understood that it is necessary to have spiritual strategies before organizational structures. At times the reorganization focuses on staff. At other times it focuses on the governance structures. Seldom does it focus on sharpening strategies to help congregations reach their full kingdom potential.

3. Too many denominations use allocation approaches to solve financial crises rather than innovative approaches. They keep dividing the financial pie rather than figuring out a way to bake a different pie. They have an inadequate fund development philosophy and strategy. They fail to realize and act on strategies that help congregations develop greater generosity or financial discipleship among the people connected with them. The indirect impact of innovative approaches is congregations which invest in the fund development vehicles of their denomination.

4. The types of Programmatic Emphases many denominations attempt involves getting as many congregations as possible to sign up for a certain project or emphasis. They are trying to show the value of the denominational efforts rather than to increase the value of congregations. A better approach is to discover what type of spiritual and strategic approach will assist each congregation in taking the next steps in ministry within their context and their current stage of development.

5. Some national denominations have become experts at dividing and driving away congregations and adherents by badly addressing explosive moral and theological issues. The big moral ones these days focus around sex—homosexuality, adultery, promiscuity, and pedophilia. When national denominations combine these with issues around clergy ordination and discipline—or lack thereof—it creates an "ensmallment" [rather than enlargement] movement within the denomination.

Typology of Denominational Organizations

Over a lifetime of observation and working with denominational organizations either in staff roles or as a consultant/coach, I have observed seven types of denominations. Some of these categories have *FaithSoaring* Denominations who function in the category, some have denominations who are trying, and some have no evidence of *FaithSoaring*. Which one of these denominational types is most like your denomination? These types are presented alphabetically.

Emerging Denomination: This is a denomination, or a region or judicatory within a denomination, which was organized during the last 15 years, or has experienced a radical restart in the past 10 years, and is significantly empowered by its current vision. It is probably focusing on one of several emerging models for denominational organizations. Very likely its focus is highly congregational in nature with a particular focus on Perfecting and Pursuing Congregations which were referenced in chapter one.

Institutionalized Denomination: This is a denomination, or a region or judicatory within a denomination, which focuses on the institutions, programs, and management aspects of being a denomination. It seeks to build long-term loyalty to the denominational organizations, and uses this as a test of fellowship for ministers and congregations. Rather than focusing on congregations, it focuses on the denomination. It is, therefore, using a 20th century model of denominationalism that is fast fading.

Missional Denomination: This is a denomination, or a region or judicatory within a denomination, which has figured out how to be on a continual transformational mission that takes the denomination and its affiliated congregations into new frontiers of mission and ministry focused to address the context it serves. It seeks to engage its congregations in missional formation and missional engagement within the framework of fulfilling the Great Commission in the spirit of the Great Commandment.

Preparing Denomination: This is a denomination, or a region or judicatory within a denomination, which realizes that it has been in decline and too institutional in its focus, and seeks to rediscover congregations and prepare for a new spiritual strategic journey in the direction of its full kingdom potential. The key issue is whether or not it will be able to make enough transitions and changes to transform. It may take an external third-party who is given authority to compel that certain transitions and changes occur.

Paradenomination: This is a denomination, or a region or judicatory within a denomination, which has determined to become a paradenomination which provides products and services to and beyond its affiliated congregations, and focuses on a small, specific set of services that might appeal to various affinity groups of congregations rather than visualizing that it has a no-exit relationship with all its affiliated congregations. Those congregations who embrace the focus of the denomination are served. Those who do not, are not.

Pursuing Denomination: This is a denomination, or a region or judicatory within a denomination, which has prepared itself and is engaging in a new transformational journey. It is clearly on a new spiritual strategic journey where it is experiencing increased vitality in multiple areas. It is making obvious progress that attracts more loyalty to the denominational organization, and interest from congregations outside this organization. It is clearly focused on helping congregations engage in a transformational journey.

Surviving Denomination: This is a denomination, or a region or judicatory within a denomination, which has diminished vitality in multiple areas of emphasis, and has difficulty sustaining a resource base to support whatever mission it continues to define. It may have been through several rounds of reorganization or cut backs, and is in or approaching a permanent *cut back syndrome* situation. Their core values have changed from being the drumbeat of a movement to smothering an institution.

The Solution: *FaithSoaring* Denominations

The solution to the dilemmas and to the typology categories where *FaithSoaring* is not empowered, is to become a *FaithSoaring* Denomination. These denominations have most or all of the following 25 characteristics:

1. They start the number of new congregations each year equal to three percent or more of the number of affiliated congregations they have at the beginning of the calendar year. They exhibit a deep commitment to church planting, and understand this as both a way to renew the core while extending the ministry, and a way to fulfill the Great Commission in the spirit of the Great Commandment.

2. They have proactive and intentional approaches to evangelism that effectively focus on inviting preChristians to begin a Christ-centered, faith-based journey, and to continue to develop spiritually as they grow in discipleship. They are comfortable with and sure of their approach to evangelism. It may be an approach that is unique to their denominational culture, but it is clearly defined and is a key focus of the denomination.

3. They believe denominations exist to serve congregations. Congregations are number one. In various expressions, congregations are the basic building block of the kingdom of God. They are genuinely humble about building up congregations rather than building up the denomination. They will sacrifice drawing attention and false glory to the denomination in favor of lifting up the effective ministry service of congregations and their leaders.

4. Empowering vital and vibrant congregations is their top priority, since congregations are the basic building blocks of the sustainable work of God's kingdom. Leaders are important to develop, but best is developing leaders who are *FaithSoaring* and understand the processes and journeys needed to help congregations be *FaithSoaring*. While issues, causes, and relationships to affiliated organizations aligned with the denomination are important, they are not the priority.

5. They have a strong focus on innovative, leading edge congregations who might already be considered *FaithSoaring* Churches. They partner with them in peer learning communities to help them take the next steps in ministry. They help leading edge congregations see themselves as part of the informal enduring visionary leadership community within the denomination. Thus, they play an important role in vision casting within the denominational family.

6. They have an effective strategy for transforming congregations that uses the Spiritual Strategic Journey or Experiential Missional Journey process, or compatible processes. They are not just trying to fix congregations with cosmetic approaches, but to help congregation discover solutions to their lack of vision and ineffectiveness in their current context. They believe that helping to transform congregations is a complementary effort to the starting of new congregations.

7. They have a proactive strategy to diversify their denomination's multi-ethnic, multi-racial, and multi-cultural nature. Much, if not all, of their net growth comes from their ethnic, racial, and cultural diversity. This diversity is celebrated as congregations become more diverse, and as their church planting strategies develop specialized tracks which start congregation indigenous to various ethnic, racial, and cultural settings.

8. They are willing to make the tough decisions to help old age congregations either experience radical transformation or die leaving a legacy. They help these congregations engage in an extreme congregational makeover which can involve giving authority over to an outside third-party to compel the necessary transitions and changes within the congregation. For those congregations who choose to die, they have various avenues to help them invest remaining assets in new kingdom ministry.

9. They are experiencing a net annual increase in the number of affiliated congregations. Some congregations are leaving the denomination for various reasons and in several different ways. Some congregations are

dying. Yet, they are starting enough new congregations, or having enough new congregations affiliate with them, that they are experiencing a net growth.

10. They are moving forward with the help of an empowering Vision for the denomination's future. Vision is not just for individuals and congregations. It is also an essential part of the work and ministry of denominational organizations. *FaithSoaring* Denominations know they must be fueled and driven by an empowering Vision.

11. They have a strong emphasis on global and local missional engagement. They highlight both the Great Commission and the Great Commandment. They focus not so much on sending people and groups as they do on these people and groups being received by those to whom God is sending them. This appears to be more in the missional nature of the Church, to be received as they go forth with Good News.

12. They collaborate within their denomination with various dimensions of organizations such as regions, districts, areas, etc. They much prefer this to approaches that involve conforming and competing actions within the denomination. Conforming models require the other dimensions of the denomination to come in line with the national/international headquarters. Competing models are when there is little or no agreement on how to work together. Collaborating models help produce the synergy characteristic of *FaithSoaring*.

13. They have healthy, proactive relationship with affiliated organizations such as colleges, universities, and seminaries/divinity schools, foundations, benevolence organizations, etc. They no longer wish to control these. They desire to partner with these for the fulfillment of the denomination's God-given Vision. In many cases those affiliated organizations to which they gave roots, they now give wings.

14. They have excellent and respected staff leadership who feel a unique spiritual call to denominational service. The spiritual call to denominational staff service is a unique call within God's constellation of calls to ministry. Too many people end up in denominational staff leadership who do not exhibit an understanding of this. *FaithSoaring* Denominations are blessed with staff who see their calling and role in denominational service as a core part of God's work in their lives.

15. They have empowering leadership from their board who manage policies and empower vision, while leaving many details to staff. The boards of denominations are too often a place where people from congregations seek to re-image the denomination in their image. This can be a multi-car wreck waiting to happen. But whether by policy management approaches or other life-giving approaches, the board of a *FaithSoaring* Denomination seeks to empower Vision fulfillment.

16. They are experiencing regular inclusion of younger, visionary leadership into staff, board, and volunteer roles. The next generation of leaders is embracing the denominational movement with great passion. While some of the next generation say they do not need denominations, others are saying they do not need denominations as they have experienced them. However, they want to help transform their denomination for 21st century *FaithSoaring* service.

17. They have a high commitment to continually nurturing deep relationships with clergy and laity. They realize that the most valuable currency of the 21st century is Relationships. It is more important than any of the Programs of the denomination. To enhance and share the Relationships, they are very committed to storytelling—telling the stories of leaders and congregations who are engaging in *FaithSoaring*.

18. They have a grassroots commitment to calling out, credentialing, and deploying clergy leadership. The authority for the process is as close to the congregational dimension as the polity of the denomination will

allow. As much as their non-negotiable governance and historical polity will allow, they give permission for grassroots processes closest to the place of real ministry rather than centralized or hierarchical processes.

19.   They have an agile management structure and processes. Needed changes are made quickly and are empowering in nature. While their governance systems are appropriately deliberate, they are also as streamlined as possible. All but the essential administrative and governance steps have been eliminated so that the denominational structures may keep up with the spiritually inspired actions of congregations.

20.   They have proactive, positive processes for handling controversial theological and ethical issues. They are proactive in that they do not wait for these issues to escalate beyond a reasonable intensity of conflict, but they engage them early and systematically. They are positive in that they have worked with both staff and volunteer leaders on developing the capacity to handle diversity and challenging conflict situations.

21.   Annual income from the congregations to the denomination is growing at least at the rate of inflation. It is no longer from a single, central funding vehicle, but from various vehicles for contributing to the support of missional and institutional efforts of the denomination. This is a significant challenge in both the current denominational environment and the economic environment. In *FaithSoaring* Denominations their affiliated congregations see the value and benefit of financially supporting the work and ministry of the denomination.

22.   They have a strong emphasis on developing multiple funding streams from congregations, individuals, and various other sources. In many denominations it has been years since the core, foundational funding stream has provided 50 percent or more of the funds needed to support the work and ministry of the denomination. Many *FaithSoaring* Denominations have already been working for decades to develop multiple funding streams to support prophetic ministry.

23.   They provide flexible and quick funding for new and innovative ministries who need an infusion of resources. They are always looking for ways to fund new innovations. Agility allows them to respond quickly when it is apparent the Holy Spirit is moving in a certain direction, or a process of discernment calls for action. In these cases various resources can be deployed to respond to ministry opportunities.

24.   Their endowment and reserve funds are at least two times their annual budget. They are well organized around this funding stream, and also have an assertive investment strategy. They are wise and prudent with finances, and make sure the efforts to which they commit financial resources have solid funding. They take a long-term view of their finances to be sure they can commit appropriate funds to cutting edge work and ministry that needs to be continued, and new ministry opportunities that arise.

25.   They have multiple collaborations with other denominations, paradenominations, parachurch organizations, and businesses to resource congregations. They realize it is not reasonable or feasible for the denomination to be the sole provider of products and services to congregations, if it ever was possible. It is more reasonable for the denominational staff to be brokers of resources and strategic interpreters of the effective use of resources from whatever source.

The Future of Denominations

I am currently working with several national/international denominations and a collection of regional denominational organizations/middle judicatories surrounding the issue of transforming their movements for effective ministry service in the 21st century. I am seeking to help them discern, discover, and develop an empowering future that enables them to be *real* to the movement of congregations in their tribe. *Real* is a word I use rather than words like *relevant*. I perceive denominations must connect through *real*, genuine, authentic relationships with the movement of congregations. If they do not, they may not be long for this world.

In working with North American denominations I do not seek to tell them they must function in a certain way or else. It is important to respect the unique ethos and missional understanding of their tribe. I do try to help them understand that business-as-usual may lead towards death, at either a slow or fast pace. My challenge to them is as follows: "Is the ethos and missional understanding of this tribe sufficiently strong that it can soar into a God-led future? Or, is it diffused and/or confused to the point that this tribe needs to consider other pathways?"

I like to lay out for them a series of scenarios concerning their future around which they can pray, study, and dialogue. Out of that, we choose three around which to dialogue more deeply. Ultimately the goal is for a future story for the life and ministry of the denomination to emerge that is based on God's pull into the future. This future story then becomes a dynamic, guiding story for the journey of the denomination into God's future. It is unique for each denomination. Yet, certain principles are obvious and emerge from each story.

With the increasing number of denominational organizations with whom I am having dialogue, I have determined to devote more time and focus to sketching out some generic scenarios that are not denominationally specific. This means the scenarios have not necessarily been contextualized to Disciples, Baptists, Methodists, Wesleyans, Presbyterians, Lutherans, etc.

Here is the essence of eight scenarios on which I am currently working. I covet your critique of these, and also your modification of these scenarios. Nothing is sacred or final about any of these. The scenarios are listed in alphabetical order according to their annotated titles.

Each scenario assumes an existing national/international denomination that has reached some hinge, challenge, or opportunity point, and has developed a willingness to look positively at this past, present, and future. It recognizes that it has certain enduring cultural values that may define its ethos and its future missional movement.

For denominations, it is a time for a Macedonian call where the intended pathway for a denomination's journey may need to be changed by a new vision, a new call from God, a new urgency, and a new passion to fulfill a core mission. Without such a response, many denominations are sliding into an institutional exile from which they may never return.

In which of these do you see your denomination? How would you modify or enhance these to make them most applicable to your denomination?

Eight Scenarios for the Future of Denominations

Scenario One: Build a Series of Formal Strategic Alliances with Other Denominations, Paradenominations, and/or Parachurch Organizations

While maintaining a separate identity, the denomination builds a series of strategic alliances with various denominations, paradenominations, and/or parachurch groups that increase the capacity of their denomination to serve the missional efforts of its congregations and other congregations who choose to connect. In the airline industry an example may be the Sky Team Alliance in which Delta Airlines is a core partner. Long-term this could lead to a new form for the denomination, and perhaps even merger.

Scenario Two: Engage the Denomination in Continuous Incremental Transition and Change

Focus on an ongoing journey that seeks to make continuous incremental transitions and changes in how the denomination engages congregations and the denominational entities in high priority missional programs, ministries, and activities. Embrace actions that foundationally affirm that the priority actions of the denomination are the right ones, but their implementation needs to be continuously improved to keep them relevant and effective.

Scenario Three: Hang On as a Separate Denomination Knowing It May Need to Disband at Some Point

Remain substantially the same as a national/international denomination because it fits the perceived mission and core values of the denomination. Realize that this could mean at some point in the future the denomination might diminish to the point it may need to disband or merge out of weakness with another denomination. Set no timeline for disbanding or merging, but realize this may be the ultimate result for the denomination in this era of denominational transformation.

Scenario Four: Merge with One or More Other Denominations, Paradenominations, or Parachurch Organizations

Merge with one or more other denominations, paradenominations, or parachurch groups. Do this not out of weakness or in order to survive, but to build a greater capacity to serve in the midst of God's kingdom. Consider for merger groups from your generic denominational family and from compatible tribes.

Scenario Five: Move from Being a Denomination to a Paradenomination Focusing on a Few Priorities and the Congregations Who Embrace Those

Using its current denominational form as a beginning place, transition and change the denomination to be a paradenominational organization focused on a few priorities and those congregations and affiliates who desire to embrace these priorities. Welcome other congregations to affiliate with the new paradenomination who are not necessarily from your tribe. In this scenario regional expressions of the denomination may choose to serve broader priorities and a broader collection of congregations that those historically connected with this denomination.

Scenario Six: Move from Being an International Denomination to a Collection of Regional Denominational Organizations

Determine that the national/international expression of the denomination is no longer needed. Restructure around a series of regional denominational organizations, thus closing down the national/international operations except as regions may choose to pick up various programs, ministries, and activities currently carried out by the international office.

Scenario Seven: Relaunch the Denomination Through a Radical Redesign

Engage in a complete redesign of the denomination. Everything is negotiable. Begin with the assumption that a group of congregations from a certain tribe desires to form a new denomination and is seeking to craft the first ten years of its journey. What should be the mission, core values, vision, and intentional actions of their new denomination? What are the strategies, structures, and staffing needed to empower the mission?

Scenario Eight: Transform the Denomination Through Discontinuous Significant Transition and Change

Focus on discontinuous significant transition and change that re-evaluates everything the denomination is currently doing. Refocus on making meaningful kingdom progress in areas of high priority for your tribe. Be willing to stop doing some things—at least the way they are being done—and start doing some things that have not necessarily been high priorities. Renegotiate relationships with regions and affiliates in line with the highest priorities of the denomination.

A Closing Word

Which are the best scenarios for your denomination that will result in them becoming and sustaining a *FaithSoaring* nature? Which scenario for your denomination will best support *FaithSoaring* Churches? What can you do to help your denomination pursue this choice? Go for it.

Coaching Insights for Chapter Twelve

Personal Reflections for Learners

In what ways is your congregation connected to a denomination? Do you see your denomination as *FaithSoaring*? Why or why not?

What do you perceive your role, if any, to be in helping your denomination achieve and/or sustain a *FaithSoaring* status?

Which of the dilemmas are characteristic of your denomination?

Which category in the typology of denominations best fits your denomination?

What solutions might best work to help your denomination become or sustain *FaithSoaring*?

Your Reflections: **What are your reflections on the material presented in this chapter?**

Your Actions: **What actions do you need to take about your life, ministry, and/or congregation based on the material presented in this chapter?**

Your Accountability: **How and by whom do you want to be held accountable for taking these actions?**

Postlude

Just as there was a Prelude to this book, and 11 Interludes, there needs to be a Postlude. What I address here is what I left out of the book and what the next steps will be.

What Got Left Out?

It is hard to know what ought to be in one book and ought to be left out. An image that makes sense to me is the one of where do you cut the loaf of bread and put the remainder back in the refrigerator to save for another day. Here are a few things that got left out.

How: The primary focus of this book is to make the case for *FaithSoaring* Churches and to describe them. A small amount of focus, primarily in chapter nine, deals with how to become a *FaithSoaring* Church. But, answering the "how" question is not the primary focus of this book. It was more about the "why" and building a foundation for dealing with the "how" in ongoing dialogue through webinars and teleconferences, and the future investigation of case studies.

As stated earlier, each congregation must discover for itself what it means to be *FaithSoaring* within its unique situation. *FaithSoaring* will be different in each situation. A formulaic approach will not work. What I hope is that I have created a hunger to be *FaithSoaring*. Those congregations with the capacity to become *FaithSoaring* Churches will also have the capacity to search around until they find the journey that works for them. Those congregations who require all the details are not likely to become *FaithSoaring* Churches.

Case Studies: The book is devoid of real time case studies of actual congregations. The seven congregations introduced in chapter two are composites of actual congregations I have encountered over the past 35 years of consulting and coaching with congregations. I am very hesitant to tell the stories of actual congregations in real time. Even when I do, I call them case studies and not models. Models today can fail tomorrow. I have a friend who has written an excellent book that focuses around a dozen or so real time congregational stories. As I write this we are rushing his book into production before the case studies change too much. Already there are some pastoral leadership transitions that have occurred.

One of the next steps will be to look at some real time case studies of *FaithSoaring* Churches. But, we will be careful to say these are congregations addressing their journey and moving in the direction of *FaithSoaring*, and will be very slow to say they are *FaithSoaring*. Too often congregations are declared to have arrived in their journey when they were only at a rest stop. Declaring arrival too soon may cause congregations to stop their journey and build three tabernacles.

Prayer and Discernment: As was pointed out by several of my previewers, I did not place an emphasis in this book on prayer and discernment in a manner that is characteristic of some of my other work. That was not really intentional. Yet, I do have in the incubator a book on prayer and discernment that focuses around the 100 Days of Discernment which I have developed over the past two decades. So, stay connected for more information at a later date.

Discerning the leadership of God is an essential and non-negotiable part of the journey to become and sustain the state of being *FaithSoaring*. It is not an option, alternative, or choice. It is essential and required.

Next Steps

What is really going on is that I am working on three projects in tandem that I believe will take me at least two years to complete. These are projects around the theme of *FaithSoaring* Churches, Enduring Congregations, and Extreme Congregational Makeover. These cover the spectrum of congregations who are at least one generation old. They fit the general category of transforming congregations. Let me briefly explain each of these projects.

FaithSoaring Churches: This is the focus of the current book, webinars, and teleconferences. To following this project stay in touch with www.FaithSoaringChurches.info. The target is the up to 20 percent of all North American Protestant congregations who are *FaithSoaring* at any given time.

Enduring Congregations: This is a focus on up to 60 percent of all North American Protestant congregations who are pursuing, preparing, or providing in nature. They are pursuing being *FaithSoaring*, but they are not there at the current time. They are seeking to prepare themselves for a *FaithSoaring* journey, but are not yet ready to pursue it. They are providing solid ministry, but not trying to be much different than they have been in recent years or decades.

A core assessment for these congregations is the material I have developed in response to the question, will your congregation still exist ten years from now? This focuses on the current, short-term, and long-term vitality, vibrancy, and survivability of congregations. Keep up with this project at www.EnduringCongregations.info.

Extreme Congregational Makeover: This is a focus on the 20 to 30 percent of all North American Protestant congregations who are presiding congregations. They are chaplaincy situations, cultural enclaves, and pastoral care ministries that are highly unlikely to be different than what they are without an extreme makeover. Their only choice, other than to die slow or fast, is radical transformation.

Keep up with this project at www.ExtremeCongregationalMakeover.info.

A Closing Word

Well, that is it. Thanks for reading. Stay connected for further learnings.

May the Triune God's activity in your life and your congregation stir up within you and everyone else in the congregation the potential for being a community of unconditional love known best through Jesus Christ as our Lord and Savior.

Acknowledgments

...ultitude of heavenly hosts" have helped me refine this book. Using a CrowdSourcing approach, I invited a group of people to preview the first draft of this book and offer feedback More than 70 people accepted the challenge to preview the book during a two week period that included Christmas. It is amazing that so many people volunteered to do this, and that almost 90 percent completed the assignment in time for me to submit this book.

I am very grateful to them as it has allowed me to improve the book so that it will be more useful to various congregations and denominations. The people who previewed this book and provided feedback on a questionnaire are the following:

Stan Albright, Darren Anderson, Alan Avera, Cynthia Ballard, Bill Barker, Al Bastin, Bob Bedford, Stephen Bentley, Kay Bissette, Terry Branscombe, Howard Burgoyne, Craig Butler, Carol Cabbiness, Jim Caprell, Jerry Carlisle, Michael Cheuk, David Coatsworth, Cecil Cook, Steve Cook, Sylvia DeLoach, Beth Dobyns, Emmet Eckman III, Kenneth Eriks, Renee Ford, Paul Fraser, Larry Glover-Wetherington, Randy Godwin, Gordon Gray, Tucker Gunneman, Malcolm Hamblett, David Helms, Brint Hilliard, Norma Hook, Dottie Kaiser, Bill Klossner, Danny Langley, Dave Lee, Ralph Lepley, Jeff Long, Dani Loving Cartwright, Bill Mallernee, Emmanuel McCall, Rob McCleland, Karen McGuire, John Miller, Karen Fraser Moore, Mark Press, Dan Schomer, Mark Schulz, Kevin Schwartz, Roy Smith, Kelli Sorg, Mark Stamper, Gary Straub, Paul Strozier, Cam Taylor, Scott Taylor, Ben Vandezande, James Vehling, James Waugh, Jack Whitcomb, Robert Winburn, Brian Winslade, and Mark Wise.

Let me tell you a little more about these people:

* Half are pastors of churches. One-third are denominational staff. The remainder are in various other work and ministry positions.

* 14 denominations plus non-denominational churches are represented. These include four different Baptist groups, Christian Church (Disciples), Christian Reformed Church, Church of God, Congregational Christian, Evangelical Covenant, Lutheran, Methodist, Presbyterian, Reformed Church in America, United Church of Christ.

* 23 states in the US, three provinces in Canada, plus one from Australia are represented in the previewers. California, Georgia, Indiana, Michigan, Missouri, North Carolina, Nebraska, Ohio, South Carolina, Texas, and West Virginia had at least three previewers.

I also used quotes from various ministry colleagues: Dick Hamm, John Bost, Leonard Sweet, Rick Smyre, and T. J. Addington.

I appreciate editorial assistance from Amanda Phifer of Columbia, SC, and the design of the cover by Josh Brickey of Columbia, SC.

I am appreciative of Brad Lyons, president and publisher, and the staff of Chalice Press at www.ChalicePresss. com and their Lucas Park Books imprint at www.LucasParkBooks.com for expediting the production of this book.

Finally, I want to acknowledge my thanks for thousands of congregations I have visited over the past 35 years or who have been in various audiences where I have spoken. I have learned so much from you about what makes up *FaithSoaring* Churches.

About George Bullard

[Georg]e Bullard is a Ministry Colleague and the Strategic Coordinator with The Columbia Partnership. He is also [exec]utive director [General Secretary] of the North American Baptist Fellowship of the Baptist World Alliance. He [is th]e author of **Pursuing the Full Kingdom Potential of Your Congregation** and **Every Congregation Needs a [Lit]tle Conflict**, both published by Chalice Press of St. Louis. With Chalice Press he is the Senior Editor for the TCP [L]eadership Series which includes more than 25 books.

The Columbia Partnership is a non-profit Christian ministry organization focused on transforming the capacity of the North American Church to pursue and sustain Christ-centered ministry. For more information about products and services check out the web site at www.TheColumbiaPartnership.org, send an e-mail to Client.Care@TheColumbiaPartnership.org, or call 803.622.0923.

CPSIA information can be obtained at www.ICGtesting.com
Printed in the USA
LVOW032153010212

266636LV00003B/2/P